Muskets, Knives and Bloody Marshes

THE FIGHT FOR COLONIAL GEORGIA

by

Judson J.Conner

Introduction by Buddy Sullivan

The Saltmarsh Press, Inc
St. Simons Island, Georgia
2001

Printed and bound in the United States of America.

The Saltmarsh Press P.O. Box 20032 St Simons Island Georgia 31522

Muskets, Knives and Bloody Marshes The Fight for Colonial Georgia

ISBN: 0-9666365-4-6 LC Catalogue: 00-133446

Second Printing 2002

Printed in the United States by:
Morris Publishing
3212 East Highway 30
Kearney, NE 68847
1-800-650-7888

To my comrades in arms who served their various homelands throughout the ages.

Contents

INSERTS

MAPS

INTRODUCTION

The events of the summer of 1742 might, with very little argument, be construed as encompassing one of the true defining periods of Georgia history—perhaps even that of the entire American colonial period. That eventful summer was the culmination of a unique chain of circumstances upon which the destiny of the new colony depended.

England and Spain were at war in 1742 and, for the new Georgia colony established only nine years before by General James Edward Oglethorpe, the military picture was particularly bleak. Oglethorpe's English forces had been driven from Florida two years earlier in 1740 following an abysmally poor performance at the siege of St. Augustine. Now, the proverbial hounds were baying at the door—Oglethorpe's strategically critical outpost at Frederica on St. Simons Island was under the threat of imminent invasion by a Spanish force which vastly outnumbered his own. By the summer of 1742, it had become entirely conceivable that Oglethorpe's colonial experiment in Georgia was doomed to failure. Everything seemed to point to the British expulsion from Georgia by the Spaniards.

A lesser man than Oglethorpe might well have folded his tents at that point and conceded the cause as lost. Oglethorpe was already under criticism from elements of the governing Georgia Trustees for the debacle at St. Augustine. The confidence of the remaining English forces in Georgia had been badly shaken. Morale was not high. The redoubtable Scottish Highlanders of Darien, with a reputation as the finest fighting men in the world, had been decimated at Fort Mosa.

But if defeat had come to the English on Oglethorpe's watch, so too came deliverance. As events would prove, and as described so authoritatively in this outstanding narrative of Oglethorpe and the War of Jenkins Ear by Judson Conner, the tide of history would dramatically turn on the outcome of a seemingly insignificant little skirmish on the south end of St. Simons Island, which came to be known as the Battle of Bloody Marsh.

Modern-day history books treat the events associated with Bloody Marsh as relatively inconsequential. Outside of military studies of the period, Bloody Marsh merits little more than a footnote in accounts of United States history, if even that. Georgia histories provide only a little more treatment. Without a proper analysis of the events of 1742, a good argument might be made for the seeming insignificance of the occurrences at places such as Gully Hole Creek, Bloody Marsh and Frederica. But from an analytical approach to this little-known commercial war emerges an increasing awareness of the real importance of these events. As these pages of Judson Conner's account of the War of Jenkins Ear unfold, the reader will experience a much greater understanding (and appreciation) for the difficulties and problems encountered by both English and Spanish forces. Also emerging with freshness and clarity will be a fresh understanding of the unique requirements attendant to eighteenth century warfare on Georgia's colonial coast.

Bloody Marsh becomes much more than the inconsequential little tactical victory scored by the force of English regulars and Highland Scots over their Spanish rivals, as portrayed in many history books. Bloody Marsh becomes, in the greater strategic sense, an outcome which saved a colony for Oglethorpe. Perhaps it is even no exaggeration to say that Bloody Marsh preserved an empire for England—for if Georgia had fallen might not Charleston and the Carolinas also become a tempting target for Spanish military conquest? The "ifs" accumulate with increasing frequency as this account unfolds—but that is the mystique of history, and precisely why its lessons are so important.

In this fascinating account, we learn of the events which encompassed the founding of the Georgia colony, the fortification of St. Simons Island and the efforts of Oglethorpe to establish a permanent, if shaky, foothold on the disputed Georgia coast. The major premise of the establishment of Georgia was military in nature. Oglethorpe was to provide a strategic buffer between the resentful and increasingly angry Spaniards in Florida and the energetic new commercial empire then developing rapidly in the British colonies of North and South Carolina.

Thus, the focus of this study is military in nature, and rightfully so. Judson Conner provides new insights on eighteenth century military tactics and how they were applied to the unique circumstances of war on the sub-tropical barrier islands of Georgia and upper Florida. We also learn intriguing new insights that shed new light on the increasingly acrimonious diplomatic affairs between England and Spain during the period, as well as the military campaigns of 1740 and 1742. This is particularly true as regards the events associated with Bloody Marsh. Several old concepts are effectively challenged by Conner through careful analysis of primary source materials. His book is both a good read and highly informative.

Throughout this narrative, the figure of James Oglethorpe increasingly emerges as the dominant figure of those dramatic occurrences of the little colonial war between England and Spain in the Georgia territory in 1740-42. Certainly the force of Oglethorpe's personality and the vision of his military engineering skills were the primary instruments of the salvation of Georgia as an English province. Without the dynamism of an individual such as Oglethorpe, there would have been no Georgia. Unfortunately, history does not accede proper credit to Oglethorpe in most instances. But a good argument may be made for Oglethorpe's having the greatest influence over the establishment, then survival, of any of the founders of England's other twelve North American colonies.

Certainly Oglethorpe's training and skills in the military arts were critical in the conduct of the affairs of the Georgia colony during those formative years. Over the vociferous objections of the Spanish authorities in St. Augustine, Oglethorpe expanded the English defensive perimeter southward from Savannah to the St. Marys River. The ambitious project to fortify St. Simons Island to protect British interests in Savannah and Charleston was, in every sense of the word, the last straw for Spain. Oglethorpe knew this in advance. In order to solidify his defensive position on the Georgia coast, he needed to test the will of his Spanish rivals. When the commercial war with Spain came, as he knew it eventually would, Oglethorpe was ready—he immediately seized the initiative and attacked the Spaniards at their home base at St. Augustine.

When English fortunes fell with the unsuccessful attempt to reduce St. Augustine, it was largely through the will of Oglethorpe which enabled the Georgia Trustees to carry on and continue their efforts at colonization. A lesser man than Oglethorpe might have given up and returned to England. It is to his credit, and the subsequent salvation of Georgia, that he did not.

The first seventeen years of the Georgia colony were predicated largely on military considerations due to England's difficulties with

Spain. When the war ended in 1748 and the military pressures were ended, at least for the time being, Georgia's focus turned in other directions. Slavery was legalized in the colony in 1750, which led to the development of large-scale agricultural operations along the Georgia tidewater during the two and a half decades leading up to the American Revolution. By 1776, Georgia had assumed a position of prominence—commercially, agriculturally and economically—among her sister colonies along the Atlantic seaboard. None of this would have been possible were it not for the events of 1740-42, in which Oglethorpe and his English and Scottish forces preserved a struggling new colony and enabled it to establish the foundation of its English-speaking future for the generations to come.

This book tells that story and tells it well, with authority, candor and objective readability tinted with fresh insights and new possibilities.

BUDDY SULLIVAN
Sapelo Island, Georgia
April 2000

FOREWORD

MORE THAN TWO and half centuries ago two battles were fought on the small island of St. Simons off the coast of Georgia. They were not large battles by today's standards, but in those days the future of vast tracts of territory was often determined by relatively small engagements. The Battles of Gully Hole Creek and Bloody Marsh decided whether England or Spain would be master of the American coast north of Florida. Their far-reaching effects place them among the decisive battles of American military history, and they also hold the distinction of being two of the most poorly documented battles fought in North America. To a considerable degree, fanciful legend arising many years after these events has shrouded the truth of what actually took place.

Here we seek to dispel the confusion by recounting the events of the encounters relying exclusively on reports written by those involved the struggles shortly after their conclusions. We have consulted other sources to outline the events occurring before and after the Spanish invasion of St. Simons Island and to more accurately portray the combatants, but only primary sources, drawn from both sides, were used to describe the campaign itself. Where the English and Spanish versions differ, reconciliation was sought, although the two versions are remarkably similar. Adjustments were also made to reconcile discrepancies in dates stemming from the fact that the Spanish documents were based on the Gregorian calendar, while the English reports used the Julian.

The greatest challenge was not in adjusting differing versions, but rather in filling in gaps in the narratives. The essential particulars are all there in contemporary reports, but many of the connecting events were neglected. Linkages have been supplied where necessary to sustain the narrative, and these linkages rest on imagination rather than recorded fact, but in all cases they are based on military logic and the demonstrated reaction of soldiers facing similar circumstances on other fields of strife. For example, we describe the panic that ran through the company of British regulars at Bloody Marsh in greater detail than that furnished by contemporary writers, simply because the spread of panic in military units tends to follow well defined paths. Using this approach, we have developed a narrative of the St. Simons campaign that flows logically, encompasses known facts, and provides a comprehensive picture of what transpired. Nevertheless, a certain number of unanswered questions remain, questions concerning, for the most part, "why" rather than "what." We suggest possible answers to these questions, but the reader is invited to form his, or her, own opinion. Similarly, the comments in the final chapter concerning the strengths and weaknesses of the opposing commanders are purely subjective and open to debate.

Judson J. Conner
St. Simons Island

CHAPTER I

THE INVASION FLEET

ON THE 5TH of July, 1742, a Spanish fleet gathered off the coast of Georgia, formed line of battle, and headed for St. Simons Sound. It carried an army bent on destroying the Georgia colony and laying to waste the plantations of South Carolina. It was an expedition of vengeance to restore Spanish authority over lands occupied by English colonists, and its first objective was the fortified island of St. Simons. Waiting on that island was General James Oglethorpe and a motley group of badly outnumbered defenders. However, in spite of the disparity in numbers, the odds appeared decidedly on the side of the British that July afternoon, for they held a strong position dominating the entrance to the sound.

The channel leading into the sound was, and still is, a narrow stretch of water, subject to strong currents, that sweeps to within one or two hundred yards of the southern tip of St. Simons. On that point of land, two companies of British regulars manned a series of fortifications, known as Fort St. Simons, which mounted batteries of twelve and eighteen pounder cannon. The width of the channel required the attacking fleet to approach single file. Not only would each ship be badly out gunned as it passed the fort, the defenders held the additional advantage of firing from stable gun platforms at known ranges.

The Spanish move was obviously a risky enterprise, one that must have appeared downright foolhardy to the English Red Coats standing by their great guns, but Don Manuel de Montiano, the Spanish commander and Governor of St. Augustine, had little choice but to make the effort. His attempts to land on the seaward side of St. Simons Island had been frustrated by high surf and shifting sandbars. Now, with drinking water running low, he had a choice of running the gauntlet of British guns to attain a sheltered landing site or of aborting the expedition.[1] The first alternative was most hazardous; the second was unthinkable.

As the first Spanish warship came within range, the English guns roared out in a thundering salvo, and a great cloud of black smoke billowed over the water. For two hours the battle raged: sponge, load, re-lay, fire! Gunners worked furiously in the July afternoon heat as, one by one, the Spanish ships plunged into the cauldron of fire, and. . . .

INCREDIBLY, NOT A SINGLE SPANISH SHIP WAS SUNK![2]

Casualties were few, damage was light, and by day's end the Spanish army was landing on Gascoigne Bluff, well inside the sound. Here on this small island on the Atlantic coast, the fate of Georgia and the future of the southern English colonies would be determined during the next eight days. Participants in the upcoming struggle would number less than four thousand, but the outcome of their dispute would be decisive and ultimately affect the future of millions.

❖   ❖   ❖

CHAPTER II

IN THE BEGINNING

THE FIRST EUROPEANS in the southeast part of what would become the United States were the Spanish. Early in the 16th Century, long before any other Europeans had settled in North America, Spanish conquistadors had explored the coast and penetrated deep inland in their search for fame and fortune. Ponce de Leon visited several sites in Florida in his fruitless search for the Fountain of Youth. Hernando de Soto led a Spanish expedition of over 600 men in a long trek through the southeast of the continent, a journey that lasted three years and touched upon no less than eight future states: Florida, Georgia, North and South Carolina, Tennessee, Alabama, Mississippi, and Arkansas. But he found no gold and discovered no rich cities, so Spanish interest flagged as colonial officials concentrated on exploiting the riches of Mexico and South America.

That interest was suddenly rekindled in 1564 when a settlement of French Huguenots, led by Jean Ribault, was established at the mouth of the St. Johns River, the waterway that empties into the Atlantic Ocean at present-day Jacksonville. The Spanish reacted immediately and violently, for not only was this an encroachment on Spanish-claimed territory, it also represented a dangerous threat to Spanish shipping lanes. Galleons carrying treasure to Spain from the Caribbean sailed northward along the Gulf Stream before picking up the westerly winds that brought them across the Atlantic, and that Gulf Stream skirted the coast of Florida.

That same year, King Philip of Spain ordered Pedro Menendez de Aviles, an enterprising Spanish nobleman, to establish a Spanish outpost in Florida and eliminate the French settlement.[1] Menendez complied thoroughly and brutally, and from his newly established base of St. Augustine, he set in motion a missionary effort to enlighten the Indians living along the coast and to reinforce Spanish claims to the area. Begun by the Jesuits and later carried to completion by the Franciscan monks, the missions were planted at coastal

Indian villages as far north as Port Royal, South Carolina. By the middle of the 17th Century, these missions numbered upwards of seventy,[2] each presiding over a settlement of Indians engaged in farming and practicing Christianity. As in other missionary efforts, the sword followed the cross, and a small but visible military presence further enhanced Spanish claims. By the middle of the 1600's, however, Spain was no longer the only European power in North America. English colonies dotted the middle coast, and France controlled a great arc of territory stretching up the St. Lawrence River, along the Great Lakes, and down the Mississippi to the Gulf of Mexico. There was also an active French trading post at the mouth of the Mobile River. European settlers and traders naturally carried national animosities with them to the New World, and where they met, there was bound to be friction. The Indians were drawn into the fray on one side or another, but they entered the contest eagerly, for they too had old scores to settle with one another.

Beginning about 1650, the Spanish missions along the Georgia and South Carolina coasts started a slow but steady decline. The reasons for this deterioration were varied and dissimilar, but they reinforced one another. Christian Indian populations declined as their members drifted back into the interior or succumbed to diseases brought to the New World by the very ones who had come to enlighten them. Pirate raids also took their toll, for this was the golden age of piracy, and French and English corsairs were numerous and bold.[3] There was also pressure from unconverted Indian tribes living in the interior, which greatly increased after 1670 when the English colony of Charles Town (Charleston) was established. The newly arrived Englishmen not only encouraged the natives to menace the Spanish missions, they provided the Indians with new and more lethal weapons to carry out the harassment. The peaceful Indians who had embraced European ways were simply unable to resist the muskets, iron tomahawks, and tempered knives of their warlike brethren.

The Spanish reacted strongly to the British threat. They began construction on the Castillo de San Marco, the fortification designed to discourage attacks on St. Augustine and provide a refuge for its citizens in time of war. They also launched an unsuccessful attack to eliminate the new English colony in 1686.

During the final third of the 17th Century, the Spanish mission network continued to dwindle and to undergo a series of consolidations and relocations. By the end of the century, not a single Spanish mission was left north of what is now the state of Florida. This did not mean that Spain had abandoned her claim to this emptying coastline, but the English considered the Spanish claim debatable and referred to that portion of the coast as the "Debatable Land." They contended the Altamaha River was the logical southern boundary of the English settlements.

Here it should be noted that colonial conflicts between nations were but extensions of greater disputes, which erupted from time to time, and which were settled, for the most part, in the European arena. Outcomes of events in the New World settlements were inevitably linked with the fortunes of the mother countries in Europe and on the high seas. And Europe and the high seas enjoyed a much higher priority than colonial America in the scheme of things.

It was during Queen Anne's War (1702 –1713), one of a series of Anglo-French conflicts over colonial and maritime interests, that Charleston and St. Augustine exchanged blows. Spain was allied with France, and in 1702 a British force captured and burned the town of St. Augustine, but failed to take the Castillo.[4] Then four years later a combined French and Spanish expedition was launched against Charleston, but the English settlement survived intact.[5]

With peace restored between the mother countries, the contest for control of the Debatable Land still continued to simmer. The next move in the colonial game was made by the English settlers in South Carolina. In 1721 they built a fort at the mouth of the Altamaha River. which consisted of a 26 foot square, three-story blockhouse with overhanging upper floors surrounded by an earthen wall and stockade. Named Fort King George, in honor of English King George II of England (1727 – 1760), it was garrisoned by His Majesty's Independent Company of Foot,[6] a limited-duty outfit numbering a hundred men. The company was recruited from a British "invalid" regiment, composed of troops too old or physically unfit to perform line duty, but capable of being garrison soldiers. These invalid units were, in a sense, the 18th Century version of military retirement.

Needless to say, Spain lodged a series of strong protests over the presence of Fort King George on what was obviously Spanish land, but other commitments precluded direct military action and her protests were ignored. Ironically, the establishment of the fort was not directed against the Spanish, but rather the French. French traders traveling up the Mobile River to its headwaters in the highlands of Georgia and Alabama were becoming increasingly active among the Indian tribes of the area. Since the headwaters of the Altamaha also drain this area, the South Carolinians were convinced it was only a matter of time before the French realized the advantage of shipping

THE INDIANS

Indians played important roles in all the colonial wars. They were not fitted—by weaponry, organization, or inclination— to stand and slug it out with organized troops, and they seldom tried. Rather they specialized in "guerrilla warfare," hit and run tactics, sudden overwhelming assaults and withdrawals. They were very good at this, for their stealth, mobility, and knowledge of the environment allowed them to choose the time, place, and duration of combat. Colonial forces traveling through hostile Indian territory were largely blind to anything beyond their immediate vicinity, while the European allies of those Indians knew all that occurred there. Because of their ability to provide and deny intelligence, Indian allies were sought by all the European countries contesting the control of North America, and the Indian warriors were most effective when coupled with European forces. During the Spanish campaign on St. Simons Island, Indians allied with the British completely outclassed those who accompanied the Spanish, and they played an important part in the English victory.

❖   ❖   ❖

furs down the Altamaha to the Atlantic coast, rather than via the Gulf of Mexico, thereby significantly shortening the ocean voyage to France. A French outpost at the mouth of the Altamaha River would be most detrimental to English interests, so Fort King George was established there as a precaution.

As it turned out, neither the French nor the Spanish ever attacked Fort King George, but its garrison, nevertheless, suffered appalling casualties. In the fort's first year of existence, no less than 65 men—two thirds of its total garrison—perished from disease, mostly from malaria. Replacements were sent and the death toll continued to rise until 1727 when the garrison was withdrawn, except for two lonely observers, left in place to maintain a British presence. In all, 140 men had died. On a per capita basis the occupation of Fort King George resulted in more fatalities than any other American military venture.

The anticipated French threat failed to develop.[7] Their relations with the Indians turned sour, and the French traders were never able to forge the trade network they sought. South Carolinian fears abated, but animosity against

the Spanish remained high, fanned by the Spanish policy of protecting run-away slaves. Initially Spanish authorities agreed to compensate English plantation owners for slaves who fled to Florida, but little was ever paid. Eventually all pretense of cooperating with English slave owners was dropped. A slave who reached Florida was free, and South Carolinian slave owners chaffed over the quite literal flight of their capital.[8]

Carolina Indians were sent south to raid Spanish settlements, and the Spanish responded in kind. The Yamasee Indians, a sub-tribe of Creek Indians living in South Carolina, had been defeated by the English settlers and driven from their homes in 1717. Fleeing south to be embraced by Spanish hospitality, they eagerly enlisted in the anti-English crusade orchestrated by the governor of Florida.

Needless to say, the South Carolinians were among the strongest advocates for the establishment of another English colony in the Debatable Lands, and when at last it came about, they loudly applauded and pledged their support. The new colony was named Georgia, after King George II, and the colonists were led by a man of great energy, ability, and stature: James Edward Oglethorpe.

❖   ❖   ❖

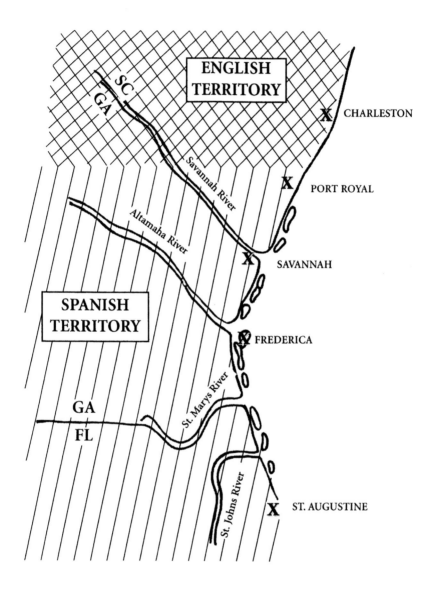

SPANISH CLAIM, 1740

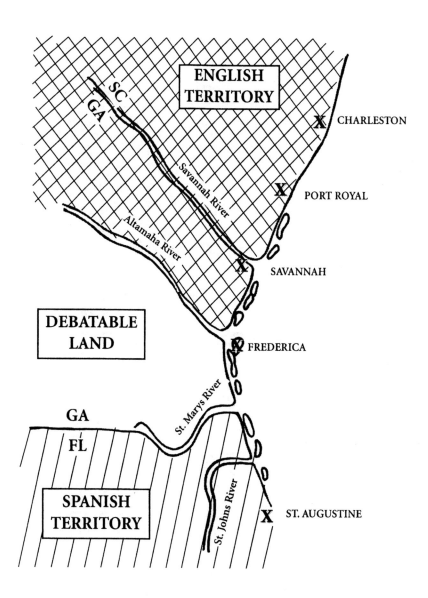

ENGLISH CLAIM, 1740

James Edward Oglethorpe

CHAPTER III

THE GEORGIA COLONY

THE COLONY OF Georgia was founded in 1732 with the establishment of the town of Savannah on a bluff overlooking the river of the same name. The settlement was unique inasmuch as it was not a crown colony; that is, it was not headed by a governor appointed by the King and answering only to the government of Great Britain. Instead it was governed by a board of trustees, an association of well-to-do English gentlemen who launched the enterprise for philanthropic, commercial, and patriotic reasons. Its purposes were three in number: to provide a refuge and fresh start for inmates of English debtor prisons; to be a profitable business investment; and to provide a buffer between the English colonies to the north and the Spanish settlements in Florida. As it turned out, few debtors ever came to Georgia, and the trustees lost money on the undertaking. Only the third goal was achieved, and it is here we direct our attention. In passing, it is interesting to note that the trustees sought to create a healthier social atmosphere by banning three things from the colony: hard liquor, slavery, and lawyers.[1] These bans proved difficult to enforce, however, and by the time the colony reverted to crown control in 1752, all three had infiltrated the settlement.

Only one of the trustees ever came to Georgia, and that was the leader of the colonists, James Oglethorpe—soldier, parliamentarian, nobleman, reformer. He was an excellent choice for the position because he was a man of great stature, boundless energy, and driving determination. He was also young for the position he held, only 36 years old when the colony was established.

James Edward Oglethorpe was born into a noble English family of considerable means and influence. As a member of Parliament, he became a knowledgeable and outspoken critic of the English penal system. It was only natural he should take a keen interest in the Georgia Colony, since one of the purposes of that settlement was to alleviate the overcrowding of debtors' prisons. He became one of the trustees who governed and largely bankrolled the colony, and the Board of Trustees chose him to lead the enterprise.

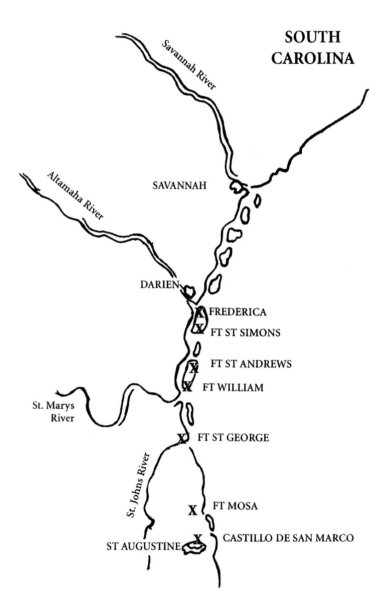

SOUTH
CAROLINA

Savannah River

Altamaha River

SAVANNAH

DARIEN

FREDERICA

FT ST SIMONS

FT ST ANDREWS

FT WILLIAM

St. Marys
River

FT ST GEORGE

St. Johns River

FT MOSA

CASTILLO DE SAN MARCO

ST AUGUSTINE

FLORIDA

THE MILITIA

As in other colonies, all able-bodied Georgia men were required to maintain arms and serve in the militia. Regular drill periods were prescribed, but throughout the colonies these training sessions varied in character from worthwhile military exercises to gala social gatherings, depending on the stature of the leader and the perceived danger to the community. Thus, militia units varied widely in effectiveness and generally fared badly when pitted against regular army professionals, in spite of American folklore to the contrary. However, the militia was not intended to stand up against regular troops. Rather it was originally organized to provide protection against Indian raids, and in this capacity it served the colonies well. It also performed the important mission of providing a reservoir for various provisional units organized, equipped, and trained to carry out specific military tasks. Many of these temporary "colonial regulars" served with distinction with, and against, regular army units.

During the Spanish invasion of St. Simons, Oglethorpe's militia soldiers were used to flesh out provisional units and guard the ramparts of Frederica when other forces were operating afield. In a sense, the Darien Highlanders were militia, since soldiering was not their full time profession. But these Highlanders, who were every bit as good as the British Red Coats, were exceptions to the rule.

Oglethorpe brought to the task a great reservoir of enthusiastic energy and determination. He was also an accomplished diplomat, a quality that served him well, not only in his dealings with the Indians, but also in his efforts to bind together the diverse peoples who made up the Georgia colony. A man of imposing stature and strong character, Oglethorpe played a key role in holding the colony together during its difficult early years, and in so doing earned an honored position in American history.

Soon after the founding of Savannah, Oglethorpe moved to occupy and defend positions further south. The grant for the Georgia colony named the Savannah River as the northern boundary and the Altamaha River as its southern limit. To secure the mouth of the Altamaha, Oglethorpe settled a colony of Scots there under the leadership of John MacIntosh. They were a tough, hardy lot, these Scots, totaling some 177 men, women, and children. Though professing loyalty to the British crown, they had no particular love for the English people. However, they carried a greater animosity toward the Spanish. They first named their new settlement New Inverness, but later changed it to Darien in memory of a Scottish settlement of that name on the coast of Panama, which had been wiped out by the Spanish in 1697.[2] Oglethorpe treated the Scots as equals and wisely left them alone, thereby winning their respect and loyalty. They were to contribute heavily to the British cause in the years to come.

Oglethorpe's ability to deal with and elicit the loyalty of diverse peoples was further demonstrated by the excellent relations he forged with the Indians. The important local chief Tomochichi became his friend, and his skillful negotiations with the inland tribes won him their support, or at least their neutrality, during the upcoming struggle with the Spanish. Only the Yamasees remained committed to Spain.[3]

In addition to the fort manned by the Scots at the mouth of the Altamaha, Oglethorpe constructed a pair of fortifications on St. Simons Island, once the site of a Spanish mission of that name. In a sense it too was on the north bank of the Altamaha River. That river actually emptied into the coastal waters at Darien, but its waters met the sea only after traversing the tidal inlets separating a number of barrier islands. St. Simons was the southernmost of this group of islands, and it was here that Oglethorpe anchored the defenses of the Georgia colony.

In 1736, he built a fortified town on the western shore of the island, nine miles southeast of Darien and named it Frederica in honor of Frederick, the Prince of Wales and heir to the British throne. A substantial breastwork of earth and timber ten feet tall surrounded the town on three sides, enclosing an area of 40 acres. The wall was anchored on the Frederica River, which formed part of the inland waterway, and earthen redans strengthened the corners. A six-foot moat, flooded at high tide, skirted the outer edges of the breastwork, and two six-foot stockade fences flanked the moat. The thick woods, which blanketed most of the island, were cleared to a distance of perhaps half a mile to provide a field of fire for those manning the battlements.

Within the town walls on a bend of the river was an inner bastion, so situated that any ship approaching the settlement was forced to turn bow-first toward the fortress batteries while its side-mounted cannon pointed impotently to the flanks. The bastion consisted of massive sides, wide gun bearing battlements, and two large warehouses. It too was surrounded by a moat. Much of the construction was of tabby, the remarkably durable "concrete" of the colonial south, consisting of a mixture of water, sand, oyster shells and lime.

THE BRITISH SOLDIER

Like their counterparts in other European armies, British enlisted soldiers came from the lower classes of society. Few of them could read or write. Aptitude requirements were largely nonexistent, and so were physical requisites, apart from the need to have at least two opposing teeth to bite off the ends of musket cartridges. Proficiency of regular army soldiers depended upon how well they were led and their degree of training. Training consisted almost entirely of close order drill and mastery of the multiple steps involved in the loading and firing of the musket. It fostered unit cohesion, developed steadfastness, and achieved a rapid rate of fire, all of which set regulars apart on the battlefield. But aptitude of junior leaders and the time devoted to training varied from one unit to another. The discipline and conduct of Oglethorpe's 42nd Regiment of Foot left much to be desired,[i] and in terms of overall merit, it fell well short of the red-coated British legions that fought Napoleon under Wellington seventy years later.

The town of Frederica was laid out in neat, parallel streets and subdivided into building lots. Dwellings consisted of varying types of buildings ranging from crude lodgings to substantial two and three story structures built in the English style of the day and constructed of timber or tabby. Also within the town walls was a barracks large enough to hold more than a hundred men. The townsmen were carefully chosen by the trustees to assure a properly balanced community of artisans, laborers, and farmers. Regardless of their trades, however, they were all expected to build fortifications and serve in the militia. At its height, Frederica was the home of several hundred soldiers and civilians.

On the southern tip of the island, guarding the strait between St. Simons and Jekyll Islands was a defensive network known as Fort St. Simons. This position was actually a collection of small forts, gun emplacements, and firing trenches rather than a single integrated fortress. Houses for the garrison troops and their families were clustered nearby.

Connecting these southern defenses with Frederica was "the military road," stretching north and west through the forest for a distance of about seven miles. Not really a road, as we think of a road, it was rather a path designed as a thoroughfare for individuals traveling on foot or horseback. It was typical of colonial Georgia roads, which tended to be nothing more than

1742

SAINT
SIMONS
ISLAND

Gully
Hole
Creek

FREDERICA X ✕

M
I
L
I
T
A
R
Y

R
O
A
D

LONG ISL.

Bloody
Marsh ✕

ATLANTIC
OCEAN

SAINT SIMONS
SOUND

X FORT SAINT
SIMONS

JEKYLL
ISL.

0   1   2
MILES

LAND   MARSH   WATER

traces through the woods. Heavy objects, which might have traveled by wagon, were more easily shipped by boat, since most settlements were located along the rivers and inland waterways that served as the super highways for the southern colonies. This forced reliance on boats for the transportation of heavy weapons and supplies had a profound effect on military operations. It restricted the size of armies, confined their areas of operations, dictated their objectives and placed definite limits on what they could do.

To strengthen the defenses of Georgia, Oglethorpe was given a regiment of regular British infantry, formed by soldiers from England, Gibraltar, and South Carolina. Officially designated the 42nd Regiment of Foot, it was also known as "Oglethorpe's Regiment."[4] Unlike the standard British regiment which numbered a thousand men divided into ten companies, the 42nd Regiment of Foot had only six companies, totaling just over six hundred troops. Regimental headquarters was at Frederica, but the regiment itself seldom, if ever, came together in regimental mass. Detachments from the unit were used to strengthen outposts along the Georgia coast and on up into South Carolina, for Oglethorpe had been named military commander of both colonies. He also had under his command various ranger units, the Georgia militia, and a company of Highland infantry furnished by the Scots in Darien. But it was the 42nd Regiment of Foot that most provoked the Spanish and escalated tensions along the Georgia frontier. Regular troops were considered superior to colonial forces, and the appearance of a Red Coat Regiment in the Disputed Land decidedly tilted the balance of power toward England.

Needless to say, Spain reacted strongly to the English provocations, but the reaction was limited to sharp diplomatic protests. Spanish military strength in the New World was stretched thin, and St. Augustine, located on the periphery of the Spanish Empire, did not enjoy a high priority in the allocation of resources. Taking advantage of the Spanish weakness, Oglethorpe pushed further south. He established small forts on the north and south ends of Cumberland Island, claiming the Satilla and St. Marys Rivers, which reach the sea to the north and south of that island, were separate mouths of the Altamaha. He also built Fort St. George at the mouth of the St. Johns River, practically in St. Augustine's back yard. This was too much. By no stretch of the imagination could the St. Johns River be considered a branch of the far off Altamaha.

Juan Francisco de Guemes y Horcasitas, Governor of Havana and senior Spanish official in the Caribbean, dispatched a delegation to Oglethorpe demanding the removal of Fort St. George.

The delegation called attention to a section of the Treaty of Utretcht (1713) in which the English Queen Anne had accepted the boundaries of the

UNIFORMS

Regardless of where they were stationed, regular British troops were dressed and equipped to fight conventional wars, in temperate weather, on the plains of Europe. Their most versatile piece of attire was a loose fitting shirt that reached to below the buttocks and served as shirt, undershirt, and night garment. Knee-high white socks were topped by britches, which buckled below the knee, and above these was a tight fitting sleeveless vest. Black, low-cut shoes would fit either foot, and a black tri-cornered hat was worn atop a white wig or tied-back powdered hair. The outer garment, a red overcoat that came to the knees, was adorned with buttons and ornate cuffs; and it could be buttoned back, fore and aft to facilitate leg movement and display the regimental color of the lining. The regimental color of the 42nd regiment of foot was green.[ii]

1t is hard to conceive of a more impractical dress for fighting in the tangled woods of Georgia, but it must be remembered, the British soldier was dressed to fight in the open fields of Europe, against similarly clad soldiers, where the aim was not to hide, but to be seen—to be seen, and admired, and beheld in awe and trepidation.

Spanish possessions as they then existed. Oglethorpe countered by citing the Carolina Charter, in which King Charles had granted the Lords Proprietors title to lands stretching south to the 29th degree of latitude, well south of St. Augustine. However, Oglethorpe eventually agreed to abandon Fort St. George and tensions were temporarily alleviated. As for the location of the boundary between English and Spanish settlements, Oglethorpe held that it was a matter for the two home countries to decide, and he managed to arrange a treaty with St. Augustine Governor Francisco del Moral Sanchez, de Guemes' subordinate, which temporarily recognized the status quo. The status quo was decidedly against Spanish interests, and de Guemes immediately denounced the agreement. So did the Spanish king, who declared it null and void and recalled the hapless Sanchez. The following year the king appointed Colonel Don Manuel de Montiano, a career soldier, to be Governor of Florida.

Upon his arrival in St. Augustine in 1737, Governor Montiano began strengthening its fortifications in preparation for the conflict he saw looming on the horizon. Oglethorpe, too, set about building up his forces, for he confidently predicted that hostilities would soon begin. And he was right.

CHAPTER IV

THE ST. AUGUSTINE EXPEDITION

THE LONG-BREWING war between England and Spain began in October, 1739. The issue was not the location of colonial boundaries, but rather a question of trade. English merchant marine captains found trading with Spanish colonies most profitable, and it was a practice heartily endorsed by Spanish colonial merchants seeking to avoid Spanish tariffs. The Spanish government, on the other hand, took a different view and placed stringent restrictions on the trade. Frustrated English merchants were supported by the English public in demanding a military solution. Robert Walpole, the British Prime Minister, had managed to avoid war until the appearance before Parliament of an English sea captain named Jenkins. Some years earlier Jenkins had been caught trading illegally by Spanish authorities and had suffered the loss of one of his ears in an on-the-spot administration of Spanish justice. Waving his severed ear for all to see, Jenkins told Parliament that a Spanish officer had handed it back to him with the comment, "Carry this home to the King, your master, whom, if he were present, I would serve in like fashion."[1] The country howled for revenge, and Walpole had little choice but to acquiesce to popular demand. The records called the resulting conflict King George's War. Its popular name was "The War of Jenkin's Ear."

When the war began, the Spanish position in Florida was weak. Governor Montiano had at his disposal only about 600 troops to guard the frontier, man various outposts, and garrison the Castillo de San Marcos. He immediately turned to Havana for reinforcements.

Oglethorpe, with typical energy and resolve, set about organizing an expedition to attack St. Augustine before Montiano could be strengthened. However, he had to have South Carolina reinforcements to accomplish the task, and the South Carolina Assembly had to first authorize their formation and use. One delay followed another as a frustrated Oglethorpe fretted over the passage of time. At last a force of 400 South Carolina volunteers was organized under the command of Colonel Alexander Vanderdussen. Supplies were gathered and a British fleet of seven warships under the command of Commodore Vincent Pearse stood ready to support the effort. By then, however, Montiano had received an additional 200 troops and, most importantly, six "half galleys" to guard the approaches of St. Augustine.[2] These "half galleys" were oar driven, ideal for operating in narrow coastal waterways, and they carried armaments capable of challenging British men-of-war in these restricted coastal waters.

It was not until the end of May, 1740, that Oglethorpe was able to concentrate his forces—South Carolinians, rangers, Indians, Highlanders, militia, and most of the regulars from the 42nd Regiment of Foot—for the Florida campaign. He launched his attack on the last day of the month and immediately set about proving the validity of Murphy's Law. Everything went wrong.

Oglethorpe had planned for a short campaign, climaxed by a decisive battle on the outskirts of St. Augustine. However, the wily Montiano refused to play the English game. Instead, he abandoned his outposts, gathered up the citizens of St. Augustine, collected his outnumbered troops, and retired into the Castillo. Oglethorpe marched and counter marched in an attempt to lure the Spanish forces from their sanctuary, but it was no use. The Castillo was too strong to be taken by assault from the landside, but it presented a less formidable face to St. Augustine Bay. From the waterside it might have been taken after an effective artillery preparation, but a waterside assault would have required the presence of the British fleet in the bay. Commodore Pearse decided that an attempt to force an entrance to these waters would be too risky in the face of the Spanish half galleys.[3] An admiral with the boldness of the English sea captains who defeated the Spanish Armada—a Drake or a Hawkins—would probably have made the attempt, but Pearse was a cautious man.

Denied the advantage of being able to batter the water-facing fortress walls at close range, Oglethorpe was forced to conduct the bombardment from the barrier island of Anastasia, a thousand yards across the bay. Here he positioned six eighteen-pounder cannons, supplemented by eight smaller ones and a few mortars. The barrage lasted for 27 days, from the 24th of June until the 20th of July. It was largely ineffective. Some damage was done to the parapets, but at that range cannon balls were not able to penetrate the walls of the Castillo.[4] It was all very discouraging from the British point of view, but a far greater set back was suffered at Fort Mosa.[5]

Prior to opening of the bombardment, Oglethorpe had sent a sizable force to operate in the area north of St. Augustine. The large scouting party's

THE MUSKET

The standard infantry weapon of the 18th Century was the flintlock musket. Far superior to the cumbersome wheel lock, or "blunderbuss," which it replaced, the flintlock represented a major technological advance in the production of military weapons, and by the beginning of the 1700s, all major European armies were equipped with it. Together with the socket bayonet, it dictated military structure, organization, and tactics of the 18th Century.

The British version of the weapon was the Long Land Pattern Musket, better known as the Brown Bess. It weighed 12.2 pounds and fired a hefty slug of lead with a diameter of .75 inches. With various modifications, it remained the British soldier's principle weapon until well into the 19th Century. Tens of thousands of them were mass-produced and over the years found their way to all corners of the earth. As late as the 20th Century they were being fired in anger in isolated arenas of conflict.

Loading the musket was accomplished by performing a sequence of precise steps which were mastered in a timely manner only after long hours of repetitious drill. It was said that a trained soldier could fire up to five times a minute, but most of those who have ever fired a musket agree that three or four times a minute was more realistic.

Muzzle velocity of the Brown Bess was a slow (by today's standards) thousand feet per second, but the lead ball it fired weighed a full ounce and tore a gaping hole through human flesh. The weapon could kill a man at ranges in excess of 200 yards, but hitting anything in excess of 100 yards was largely a matter of chance, for the musket ball veered widely beyond that range. One contemporary observer noted that he had seen men hit at a range of 200 yards, but he had never seen anyone hit at that range by the one who was aiming at him.[iii]

mission was to harass the Spanish and to cut the overland supply line to the Castillo. An independent force such as this, operating in isolation from that main body of troops, should have been a closely-knit outfit with clearly defined command lines. Unfortunately, this was not the case. Instead, the unit was composed of seventy-odd Scots, a detachment from the 42nd Regiment, a few Indians, and about fifty South Carolinians, 137 men in all. Worse still, it was led by two commanders who detested each other. Colonel John Palmer, experienced Indian fighter and commander of the South Carolina contingent, was the senior officer, but he held a colonial commission. The Highlander commander, Captain Hugh Mackay, had a King's commission and felt no compulsion to obey the orders of a mere colonial.[6] Needless to say, the effectiveness of the force left much to be desired, but its greatest shortcoming was its failure to heed Oglethorpe's instructions concerning bivouac sites.

Since the detachment would be vastly outnumbered by the Spanish forces in the area, Oglethorpe directed that it maintain its mobility and change the location of its encampment each night. However the deserted building of the abandoned outpost of Fort Mosa, located a few miles north of the Castillo, offered a more congenial setting than the open countryside. At the end of each day the scouting force returned to it to spend the night without paying much attention to security. The practice did not escape Spanish detection, and on the night of June 25th, Montiano sent a force of 300 Spanish troops and Indians to attack Fort Mosa.

The 3:00 a.m. assault came as a great surprise to the slumbering British and rapidly turned into a slaughter. Only 25 members of the ill-fated task force managed to slip undetected over the back walls and return to the rest of the army across the bay on Anastasia Island. Spanish records indicate 35 were captured, including Captain Mackay, and the rest were killed, including Colonel Palmer. Spanish losses were light.[7]

The disaster at Fort Mosa dealt a cruel blow to British morale and aggravated the growing rift that had developed between the South Carolinians and Georgians. Part of the falling out could be attributed to unit jealousies and the ongoing rivalry between regular and colonial troops, but the disagreements also permeated the chain of command and resulted in disgruntled senior commanders. However, for all their troubles, the situation faced by the British was bright compared to that of the Spanish, who were rapidly running out of food. In another few days the Castillo would surely have been forced to capitulate, but once again fate intervened on the part of the Spain.

Commodore Pearse announced that due to the increasing likelihood of a hurricane, the British fleet would lift its blockade of the coast and depart no later than August 5th. Then on the 27th of July, seven supply ships from Cuba managed to slip through the blockade and resupply the beleaguered Spanish. Oglethorpe had little choice but to lift the siege and depart, his final decision being hastened by a threat to mutiny from a segment of his own regiment. As the disgruntled army sailed for home, it left behind 122 dead, 35 prisoners, and at least 16 deserters.[8]

THE HIGHLANDERS

The company of Scottish Highlanders recruited by Oglethorpe to establish Fort Darien at the mouth of the Altamaha River was the forerunner of the Highland Regiments that have figured prominently in the annals of British modern military history from Ticonderoga to the Falkland Islands. Its members were a hearty lot, relatively small in number, but great in effectiveness. The individual Scottish soldier wore wool stockings that came to just below the knee, a short jacket, and a tartan some eight to ten feet in length. This woolen swath of cloth was wrapped around the waist to form a kilt, then drawn up the back and fastened at the shoulder with a brooch, with the end hanging loosely along the back. In contemporary drawings it appears bulky and encumbering, but in reality it was a very practical garment. With its folds held in place along the back, arms and hands were left free to employ weapons; and on the march during inclement weather, it could be drawn up to cover the head and protect weapons. At night it turned into a warm blanket. For headgear the Highland soldier wore a "bonnet," a beret-like hat featuring a pompom on the top. He was armed with the standard British Brown Bess musket, plus an assortment of weapons of his choosing. Pistols and various knives were common, and there were also broadswords and small Scottish shields distinguished by the sharp spikes that pointed out from their centers. Known as "tiges," these shields were deadly in the hands of an expert engaged in hand-to-hand combat, which was a Highland specialty.

It has been said that the Florida campaign was Oglethorpe's school for learning to be a general. Time would tell if he had mastered its lessons, for the gods of war were arranging a rematch for him with his recent opponent.

CHAPTER V

SPANISH REVENGE

FOLLOWING THE UNSUCCESSFUL Florida expedition, criticism and recriminations flew back and forth between South Carolina and Georgia and bounced across the Atlantic to England.[1] The South Carolina Assembly condemned Oglethorpe as incompetent, and he lashed back by accusing the South Carolinians of foot dragging and of being uncooperative. He even hinted at their lack of courage. The dispute soon turned into a bitter squabble, and it was a most unfortunate one, because both colonies would soon face a common danger that called for close cooperation, a cooperation that would not materialize.

Oglethorpe's Georgia forces staggered back from Florida in sad disarray. Particularly hard hit were the Darien Scots, who had suffered the lion's share of the Fort Mosa casualties. In May of 1741, the Highland Company barely numbered 16 soldiers, and the small population of Darien included no less than eight young widows and 23 fatherless children.[2]

The 42nd Regiment of Foot was in a state of disorder. Desertions, sickness, and enemy action had badly depleted its strength and morale was at an abysmal low. The regimental executive officer, Lieutenant Colonel William Cook, quarreled with Oglethorpe and returned to England. One officer committed suicide; other officers fought duels. Indeed, the officers of the 42nd Regiment of Foot inflicted more casualties upon themselves than they suffered at the hands of the enemy.[3]

By then the War of Jenkin's Ear had merged into a larger European conflict, the War of Austrian Succession (1740—1748). When Maria Theresa mounted the Austrian throne, a complicated set of relationships among the crown heads of Europe provoked the hostilities which pitted France, Spain, Bavaria, and later Prussia, against Austria. England supported Austria, and her continental commitments soon had her resources stretched dangerously thin. Admiral Edward Vernon's ill-fated amphibious expedition against Cartagena

---

ARTILLERY

The artillery of the 18th Century fell into one of two categories: field artillery, which accompanied troops in the field, and ship-borne or fortress-mounted artillery. Field artillery, mounted on large wheels and drawn by teams of draft animals, saw little use in early colonial wars because lack of roads severely restricted its mobility, and the wooded terrain limited fields of fire. But cannons mounted on ships and in fortresses played important roles in early American warfare.

At that time the size of direct fire guns was designated by the weight of the iron balls they fired, thus an eight pounder fired a ball weighing eight pounds. Oglethorpe employed cannon ranging in size up to eighteen pounders. These were massive things weighing well over a ton, with barrels nine feet long. Although they could fire a missile more than a mile, accuracy diminished with distance. Their effective range was about a half-mile. Although they appear crude to us today, these muzzle loaded, smooth bore guns had evolved for three centuries by the early 1700's,[iv] and in the hands of experienced gunners, they could be devastatingly accurate.

---

on the Spanish coast of South America further impacted on British coffers and rejuvenated Spanish confidence. In the fall of 1741, the Spanish King decided the time was ripe to drive the English from Spanish claimed land along the coasts of Georgia and South Carolina. He assigned the task to the Governor of Havana, Juan Francisco de Guemes, and directed him to form an army and carry out an assault on Port Royal, South Carolina, which had been the site of a 17th Century Spanish mission. He left it up to de Guemes to select a commander of the expedition, and de Guemes named St. Augustine Governor Montiano. It appeared to be a wise choice. Montiano was an experienced soldier and proven administrator, and he had already beaten the British once. Additionally, a significant portion of the expeditionary force would have to come from the St. Augustine garrison, and by appointing the Florida governor commander of that force, de Guemes assured the St. Augustine contingent would be adequate in number and quality. Montiano estimated the task would require an army of three thousand. He would end up with a force barely two-thirds that size.

RANGERS

Rangers were specialized colonial troops raised to perform specific tasks. They garrisoned frontier forts, patrolled waterways, and conducted scouting and reconnaissance missions. In the pay of either the crown or various colonies, they were organized into companies of differing sizes, each commanded by a captain.[v] The several ranger companies under Oglethorpe's command fell into one of two categories: boat rangers or horse rangers. Boat rangers kept open the waterways of Georgia, escorting personnel or commerce as required. Horse rangers handled the land missions, mounted on horses they provided. They were by no stretch of the imagination cavalry. When they were required to fight, they fought on foot. Horses were for transportation only. Rangers were clad according to individual whim, normally in rough buckskin clothing, and in addition to a musket, they carried an assortment of weapons: knives, hatchets, pistols, etc. Because these ranger companies varied in size from twenty or thirty individuals to as few as three or four, it is difficult to determine the exact number of rangers on duty with Oglethorpe when the Spanish attacked St. Simons Island. Sixty or so is a logical guess, and of this number, many must have been on scouting missions or performing outpost duty when the critical battles were fought.

❖   ❖   ❖

It took six months to gather the invasion force, and during that time the initial objective was changed from Port Royal to the British fortified island of St. Simons. The Spanish did not expect much resistance from the 42nd regiment, but operations further north would be more secure if that regiment were first eliminated. Most of the invasion force was drawn from the garrison of Havana and consisted of two small infantry regiments, a detachment of engineers, some artillerymen, and a regiment of dragoons. These horse soldiers left their mounts back in Cuba, but they carried their saddles with them in anticipation of being remounted on captured English horses. The total number of the Havana contribution did not amount to more than 1,300 combatants, but de Guemes helpfully listed for Montiano the soldiers he could muster from the St. Augustine garrison.[4] All told, including a contingent of Yamasee Indians, Montiano would command an army of about 2,000 men. The Havana Governor expressed his conviction that such a force would be sufficient to "attain the end sought with happiness and without risk." The "end" he sought was the elimination of the fledgling Georgia colony and the destruction of the Carolina plantations.

de Guemes went on to point out he was retaining only 400 men for the defense of Havana and to remind Montiano that the forces being sent him were on loan only. They were all to be returned "with the least possible expenditure of time,"[5] once the objectives had been attained. It was a significant point, for it carried with it the tacit expectation that the borrowed forces would be returned in similar condition and number as they were received.

When word of the Spanish preparations reached Georgia, Oglethorpe redoubled his efforts to strengthen his forces, and he applied for help to both South Carolina and England. Still smarting over the aftermath of the Florida expedition, the South Carolina Governor and Assembly turned a deaf ear, and even the mother country refused aid. With the spread of the war to Europe, England had other, more pressing commitments to meet.[6]

Oglethorpe was on his own. Typically, he met the challenge with energy and determination.

"We are resolved not to suffer defeat. We will rather die like Leonidas and his Spartans if we can but protect Georgia and Carolina and the rest of the Americas from desolation."[7]

There was one small bright spot in the otherwise gloomy outlook that settled over Georgia. Prior to the Florida excursion, Captain Horton had been sent to England to plead for more soldiers, and he was unexpectedly successful. An additional lieutenant was authorized for each company of the 42nd Regiment of Foot, and Horton returned the middle of June, 1742, with a company of grenadiers.[8] It was garrisoned on Jekyll Island under the newly promoted Major Horton. Ironically, it would be employed elsewhere and miss the upcoming battles on St. Simons Island.

While the Georgians were cheering the arrival of the grenadiers, the Spanish expeditionary force was gathering at St. Augustine. Numbering some 3,000 men, including sailors, it set sail in 52 ships on the 20th of June and soon thereafter ran unto a violent storm. Contrary winds scattered the fleet and drove some of the smaller vessels to seek shelter from the raging seas in Cumberland Sound. Oglethorpe assumed the Cumberland Island forts were the target of the Spanish attack and rushed there with reinforcements. After narrowly escaping capture by a Spanish warship, he reached the island with two companies of regulars and his company of grenadiers. He readjusted the island defenses, abandoning Fort St. Andrew on the northern end of the

MORTARS, BOMBS, AND GRAPE

Direct fire guns throwing round iron balls were the mainstays of 18th Century artillery, but there were other types of ordinance and ammunition. Mortars were short barreled, wide mouthed cannon that lobbed projectiles onto the target in high arching trajectories. Oglethorpe employed several of them in his siege of the Castillo de San Marco. Mortars had a shorter range than direct fire guns, but they could clear obstacles that masked direct fire. They often fired explosive shells.

Explosive ammunition were hollowed-out iron balls containing black powder and fitted with a fuse which could be cut to a length that (hopefully) would ignite the powder when the projectile was just above the target. When detonated the bomb broke into flying fragments that played havoc with ship rigging and inflicted mass casualties among unprotected personnel. In the 1740's, exploding shells were finicky things to handle and fire, and their fuses did not always burn at the prescribed rate. However, their reliability and employment increased over time, and seventy years later they would be the "bombs bursting in air" of our national anthem.

Another type of artillery ammunition in use at the time of the Spanish invasion was grapeshot. These projectiles were made up of small iron shot packaged to fit into a cannon's mouth, thereby turning the piece into a gigantic shotgun. Dispersing into a deadly burst upon leaving the muzzle of the gun, these small iron balls had a limited range but were devastating to assaulting troops in densely backed formation.

island and reinforcing the ranger garrison of Fort William on the southern end. Here he left sizable detachments of regulars drawn from two different companies. When the anticipated Spanish attack failed to materialize, Oglethorpe returned to St. Simons Island, but he left a sizable force behind on Jekyll Island under the command of Major Horton. It consisted of a company of grenadiers and parts of two other companies of regulars.

Recovering from the bad weather that had dispersed their fleet, the Spanish re-assembled 34 of the larger ships, which carried most of the army. The force appeared off the coast of St. Simons on the 28th of June. It was Montiano's intention to land on the eastern shore and drive across the island to the Frederica River, thereby cutting off Fort St. Simons from the fortifications of Frederica. High surf thwarted his plans, however, and with his water supply running dangerously low, he decided to run the gauntlet of fire from Fort St. Simons to reach the calmer waters of St. Simons Sound. It would be a risky undertaking, but once in the sound, the fleet would be protected from high seas, and landing operations would be much easier. Gathering at the entrance to the inlet, the fleet waited for an east wind and a rising tide. The required conditions appeared in the afternoon of July 5th, 1742.[9]

CHAPTER VI

THE INVASION

THE SPANISH FLEET successfully forced a passage into St. Simons Sound and anchored about 5:00 p.m. off Gascoigne Bluff on the southwest corner of St. Simons Island. In spite of the heavy curtain of fire laid down by the British guns, damage suffered by the fleet was remarkably light and casualties few: four dead and nine wounded. The bluff, named for Captain James Gascoigne, who had built a small shipyard there, lay adjacent a deep-water anchorage and offered firm ground and adequate space for a landing in force. Montiano ordered the debarkation to begin immediately.

Spanish warships swept the landing site with a preliminary barrage, and the first echelon went ashore unopposed. The landing operation continued throughout the night and was completed by dawn,[1] which was no mean feat. The troops and equipment had to be transferred to shore in small boats, a task requiring considerable control, skill and coordination even in daylight. The fact that it was accomplished at night, successfully and with dispatch, speaks well of the Spanish army and its leaders.

While the Spanish landing operation was underway, the English were evacuating Fort St. Simons. Having been overtaken by events, the useless position had now become a potential trap, and Oglethorpe wisely decided to concentrate his forces at Frederica. Magazines were blown up, cannons spiked,[2] supplies put to the torch. Three of the coastal freight ships anchored next to the fort were burned, but a frigate and a sloop of war managed to slip past the Spanish and put out to sea.

The British were severely hampered in their evacuation by darkness and by restrictions imposed by the military road. Since the road would not accommodate wagon traffic, everything the English salvaged had to be carried by hand or on pack animals. By midnight the last of the departing troops were on their long, dark trek to Frederica, their departure lit by the fires of burning ships and supplies.

Contemporary portrait of Spanish fleet in the Sound.

As the last of the English soldiers departed, a party of Yamasee Indians was on its way to reconnoiter these positions. The Indians found the British gone, but several houses in the area were intact and filled with great quantities of intriguing things to loot. The quantity of plunder taken by the Indians that night apparently had a negative effect on their later performance. A Spanish observer, commenting on one of the Indian patrols sent out by Montiano to find an alternate route to Frederica, wrote: "The Indians returned like all the rest without accomplishing anything whatsoever, but we

THE SPANISH SOLDIER

Spanish infantry soldiers were equipped, clad, and organized much the same as their British counterparts, except that their regiments (sometimes referred to as battalions) were about half the size of the standard English regiment. Each contained a company of grenadiers. The two infantry regiments sent from Havana to participate in the Spanish invasion of Georgia wore white uniforms trimmed with regimental colors, red for one of the units, blue for the other.[vi] There was also a regiment of dragoons, horse soldiers trained to fight dismounted. These dragoons wore boots, green uniforms, and (in all probability) the superior expression affected by mounted troops when associated with foot soldiers. Spanish soldiers who came from the St. Augustine garrison, including at least one company of light infantry scouts, wore dark blue uniforms and the standard black tri-cornered hats that were common to most armies. As in the British army, Spanish enlisted men came from the lower classes of society, and the officers were drawn from the aristocracy.

should not be astonished that they should refuse to expose themselves, seeing that they are rich, for a few have more than six hundred dollars worth of loot."[3]

An hour or so before dawn, two companies of Spanish grenadiers were sent to take possession of the fort and prevent further destruction of property. In addition to some quantities of grenades and musket shot, they found a dozen or so cannon, many of them undamaged or improperly spiked. The fort was deserted except for two Englishmen, one of them badly wounded. There was also a dead Englishman who had been scalped by the Indians. The rest of the Spanish army came up during the morning, and the troops spent the rest of the day consolidating positions and landing supplies.

There was also considerable activity at Frederica. Women and children had been evacuated to the mainland, and the fortress town hummed with military activity as Oglethorpe collected outlying units and strengthened defensive positions. In addition to three companies of regulars from the 42nd Regiment, there was the Highland Company of forty-odd soldiers, several outfits of rangers, militia units, and perhaps fifty Indians. Also, Oglethorpe had pressed into service the crews of several merchant vessels that had moved up the river to escape the Spanish fleet. All told, Oglethorpe was able to muster from 600 to 650 men under arms, which meant he was outnumbered about three to one, or if we count the Spanish sailors, more than four to one. Pausing to assess the status of opposing forces that 6th of July, 1742, we find the English running well behind in the contest. Not only had the Spanish fleet smashed its way past the fortifications guarding the entrance to St. Simons Sound, a Spanish army had landed on the island and taken possession of the fortifications, along with some valuable ordinance.

The English had little to show for their efforts. In fact, the situation had all the earmarks of an impending British disaster. However, Oglethorpe could take consolation over a few things: Major Horton, still on Jekyll Island with his grenadiers and parts of two other companies, was actively attempting to circumvent the Spanish fleet and rejoin his commander. Guns mounted in the inner bastion controlled the water approaches to Frederica, and the parapets surrounding the land sides of the town were further strengthened by a tangled barrier of thick forest that blanketed the island. And the English Indians were the masters of that forest, a fact brought home to the Spanish the following morning when a soldier performing outpost duty was found dead.[4]

CHAPTER VII

THE PENDULUM SWINGS

ON THE MORNING of July 7th, Montiano was ready to make his next move. He knew generally on what part of the island Frederica was located, but he was unfamiliar with the terrain that separated him from it. Therefore, he sent out reconnaissance forces to scout the approach, and since he had decided to advance on two parallel routes, he sent out two patrols.[1] One was directed up the military road, which ran along the east side of the island; the other party veered westward to find a trail along the Inland Waterway. The first, commanded by Captain Don Nicholas Hernandez, was composed of 25 scouts and 40 Indians. The second patrol was a 50-man company of scouts under the command of Captain Don Sebastian Sanchez.

Sanchez and his party started out seeking a path along the western side of the island but somehow got turned around and stumbled onto the military road to join Hernandez. The combined patrols, numbering in excess of a hundred men, formed a sizable group that pushed forward in what we would call today a reconnaissance in force. Not large enough to take the objective by itself, it was still strong enough to brush aside any screening force it might encounter and either reach the objective or force the deployment of any enemy unit in its path.

The Sanchez-Hernandez task force cautiously made its way up the military road, across marshes and through the thick woods, and managed to travel about six miles before it was discovered. It is hard to conceive of the English screening network being that porous, since the English Indian allies dominated the forest. Nevertheless, the Spanish patrol arrived at the edge of a low-lying, swampy piece of land bordering Gully Hole Creek, barely half a mile from the gate of Frederica, before it was discovered. Here it ran across a party of mounted English rangers. Shots were exchanged. A ranger was hit, but his companions galloped back to Frederica and raised the alarm.

The Spanish column, which was strung out along the road for a quarter mile or more, halted. A few of the leading soldiers moved off the road to

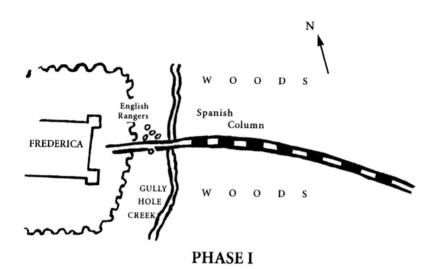

PHASE I

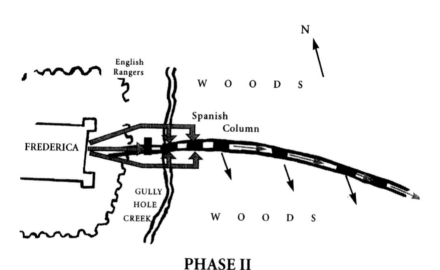

PHASE II

BATTLE OF GULLY HOLE CREEK

BATTLE TACTICS

Wars in early 18th Century Europe were fought by relatively small professional armies, and the average civilian was largely unaffected by them.[vii] To maximize the volume of fire brought to bear on the enemy, soldiers were arrayed shoulder to shoulder in tight, linear formation, and they moved about the field of combat with parade ground precision. To keep formation, employ their weapons, and withstand the withering fire of massed muskets, soldiers had to be highly trained. Such training was both expensive and time consuming, hence the paucity of citizen soldiers on the battlefield. Cities and built-up areas were also largely spared the ravages of war because proper deployment of organized forces required expanses of fairly level, open terrain. And warfare of that day and age also lacked the savagery it was later to acquire. Since trained soldiers represented a considerable national investment and could not be replaced rapidly, commanding generals were loath to squander these valuable assets. They tended to be prudent rather than rash, cautious instead of bold. Maneuver was preferred to combat, and under these conditions there was room on the battlefield for honor and chivalry and mutually understood rules. But the situation was vastly different in the New World. In the colonies open spaces were few and far between, and by the time opposing forces first discovered one another, they were often only short, lethal distances apart. Cover and concealment were more important than splendid formations. And Indians imposed their own set of rules on the battlefield, rules that were very different from the ones observed in Europe. Some military commanders adapted rapidly to the new conditions; many did not.

deploy in the tangled underbrush, and the two leaders worked their way up the line of troops to determine the cause of the firing. When they reached the head of the column, they were just short of the clearing that separated Frederica from the surrounding forest. Another hundred yards or so, another three minutes, would have placed them at the edge of the woods and perhaps have significantly changed the ensuing scenario. As it was, the Spanish force remained completely within the forest while its leaders discussed the situation and made plans to resume the advance.

When the report of the Spanish presence reached Frederica, the company of Highlanders happened to be standing in ranks, and a group of rangers and Indians were also immediately available. Additionally, a company of the 42nd Regiment of Foot was on a stand-by status, just a few minutes from being fully operational. Leaving orders for the stand-by force to follow, Oglethorpe gathered the available rangers, Indians, and Highlanders and led them in a headlong charge out the fortress gate and down the military road. It was a very rash move. Leaving a perfectly good fortress, Oglethorpe rushed out with less than a hundred men to confront what might have been the whole Spanish army. On the other hand, the approved solution to any military problem may be defined as "whatever works," and the gods of war favor the bold. On this occasion they smiled on Oglethorpe.

Captains Hernandez and Sanchez had completed their hurried conference and were just starting forward to join the lead scouts when the English fury broke into the forest and burst among them. The lead elements of the Spanish column were suddenly engulfed by a swarm of Highlanders under the command of Lieutenant Charles Mackay (not to be confused with the Captain Hugh Mackay captured at Fort Mosa). The hapless Spanish were scarcely able to get off a shot before they found themselves engaged in hand-to-hand combat with adversaries who specialized in this type of fighting. Leading the onslaught was Oglethorpe himself, who, it was said, captured a pair of Spanish soldiers single handedly.[2] The report was probably true, for Oglethorpe was a large man with a temper to match.

Spanish resistance collapsed almost immediately. Those who could extricate themselves ran back down the military road, carrying those further back along with them in a headlong dash to the rear. Some fled into the woods, but most streamed back the way they had come. The bloody affair had lasted only a few minutes, and by the time the supporting company of British regulars came double timing up, it was all over. Spanish casualties included 12 dead, 10 wounded, and 12 captured—a total of 34 men, more than a fourth of the total number of the reconnaissance force.[3] The British loses were negligible. Reportedly, only one man died, a Scot who was overcome by heat exhaustion during the run from Frederica to the field of battle.[4]

This was the Battle of Gully Hole Creek, as it was later named. The troops engaged were fewer than those who later fought the celebrated Battle of Bloody Marsh, but the casualties were greater and the results more decisive. It can be argued that Gully Hole Creek, rather than Bloody Marsh, was the turning point of the conflict. The battle marked the closest Spanish approach to Frederica and exacted the heaviest costs to both sides. The later Spanish foray resulting in the Battle of Bloody Marsh was mounted to assist the retreat of the survivors of the earlier battle rather than to threaten the English base.

Drummer, 1737-1749, Oglethorpe's Regiment of Foot ("The Old 42nd")

CHAPTER VIII

THE BLOODY MARSH

FOLLOWING THE BATTLE of Gully Hole Creek, Oglethorpe collected his forces and pusued the fleeing Spanish down the military road. In addition to his rangers, Indians and Highlanders, he had the company of regulars under command of Raymond Demere. His combined force, now numbering from 150 to 200 men, continued down the road for nearly four miles, to a point where the road broke out of the woods, narrowed, and crossed an open, marshy area before reentering the woods a hundred yards beyond. Here, on the edge of this open savanna, he placed his troops in a defensive position along the wood line. The Red Coats were positioned to the left of the road, the Highlanders on the right.[1] The left flank of the position rested on a marsh that thrusts deep down the eastern side of the island, while rangers and Indians were posted to guard the exposed right flank. It was a strong position, and it dominated the open area to its front.

Oglethorpe then decided to bring up reinforcements, and at this point he made a mistake. Instead of remaining with his deployed forces and sending for additional units from Frederica, he went back himself to get them. There is no record of the instructions he left with Captain Demere, the ranking officer, or, indeed, if he left any instructions at all.

When the commanding general left, a light rain began to fall, and Demere's men bent over their muskets to keep the priming powder dry as they stared down the path ahead. The individual soldier knew little of the overall situation, but he did know he and his comrades were outnumbered by the Spanish army, an army he could expect to come charging out of the distant wood line at any minute. Denied the comforting feeling of security afforded by a close order formation, his sense of isolation must have been further heightened by the knowledge that his leader was no longer present. Conditions were ripe for the spread of panic.

On the right flank of the position, the 42 Scots of the Darien Company viewed the situation quite differently. These Highlanders had already met the

JUNIOR LEADERS

As in modern armies, non-commissioned officers were the backbone of the 18th Century British army. A sergeant and a corporal were assigned to each platoon, and they carried out most of the day to day leadership roles. Instead of muskets, sergeants carried halyards, which were short spears with a hook and an ax extending from opposite sides just behind the tip. At one time the halyard was a major weapon on the battlefield, used to hack, thrust, or yank enemy horsemen out of the saddle. By the 1740's it had become merely a symbol of authority, but it was effective for prodding stragglers or aligning ranks.

The actual leading of the troops into battle was the job of officers, and it was considered a gentleman's task. There were a few lower class individuals who, through luck, ability or circumstance, had earned commissions; but, by and large, commissioned officers came from the aristocracy. In the British army commissions could be bought and sold, and relative rank was often a reflection of relative wealth. Because there were no military schools at the time,[viii] officer development was largely limited to on-the-job training. Yet for all his lack of formal military education, the average English officer was brave. There were exceptions, of course, but those of noble birth were expected to be courageous and set the example in combat. British officers normally did so.

Spanish in hand-to-hand combat and had beaten them badly. Surely confidence must have been present in abundant measure as they awaited another chance to avenge their countrymen lost at Fort Moosa.

When Spanish survivors of the Gully Hole Creek encounter came streaming back into the Spanish camp, Montiano organized a force to assist the withdrawal of what was left of his ill-fated patrols. He assumed, or at least hoped, his missing troops remained a coherent unit fighting a rear-guard action. The relief force consisted of two companies of grenadiers under the command of Captain Don Antonio Barba,[2] plus a few survivors of the earlier engagement who volunteered to act as guides. It was late afternoon before the column got underway.

When the Spanish relief force reached the savanna, behind which the British were waiting, it halted. The tree line in the distance somehow looked different to those who had been over the road that morning. There appeared to be outlines of barriers and brush parapets that had not been there before.[3] Barba decided to hold up the column until a reconnaissance party checked out the woods on the far side of the opening. He sent forward a platoon of perhaps 20 men under the direction of a young ensign named Don Miguel Bucardi.

The British troops held their fire as they watched the Spanish platoon file along the narrow causeway carrying the road over the marsh. They were big men, these grenadiers, resplendent in white uniforms and wearing tall grenadier hats that made them look all the more formidable. Closer and closer they came until suddenly the order was given to fire, and a resounding volley of a hundred muskets came crashing out of the woods, followed by a great billow of black smoke that rode the dense, humid air to settle over the savanna. Then three things occurred at the same time: the Spanish reconnaissance party was torn asunder, the Spanish column deployed and opened fire, and the company of British Red Coats turned and fled.[4]

The panic spread rapidly among the English soldiers. Individuals, then squads, and finally whole platoons pulled out of position and ran to the rear. A lieutenant, John Sutherland, and two sergeants ran up and down the line trying to stem the flight. They were able to stop and turn around about 25 men, but the majority of the company ran on up the military road headed for Frederica, and among them were the other officers of the company, including Captain Demere.

John Sutherland's rallied platoon eventually redeployed and joined the Highlanders in returning the Spanish fire. Both sides added to the blanket of smoke clinging to the battlefield, and both sides fired blindly at the unseen foe. The fusillades continued heavily and ineffectively for the better part of an hour until the Spanish began running out of ammunition, and Captain Barba decided to withdraw to the Spanish camp. He left behind in the marsh much of the platoon that had ventured out onto the causeway, including the fatally wounded Ensign Bucardi. The British took two prisoners. Seven of the Spanish grenadiers were killed and eleven wounded,[5] all the casualties apparently coming from the exposed reconnaissance party. No British losses were reported.

Oglethorpe was back at Frederica collecting additional forces when the battle began. When he heard the distant firing, he ordered the assembled troops to follow and galloped down the military road to the sound of the guns. On the way he met Captain Demere and his fleeing soldiers. They reported a disaster had befallen them and that Lieutenant Sutherland had

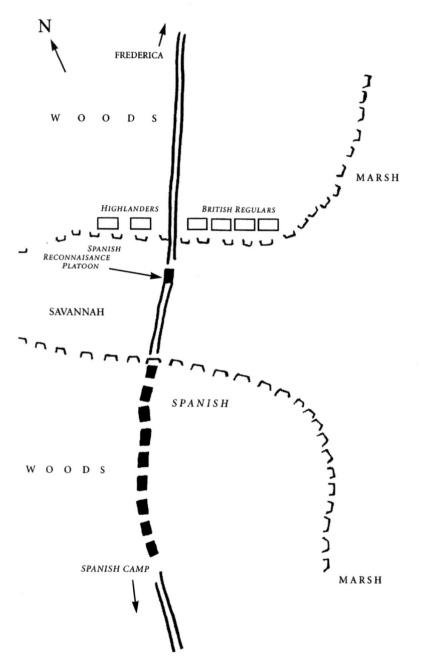

BATTLE OF BLOODY MARSH, PHASE I

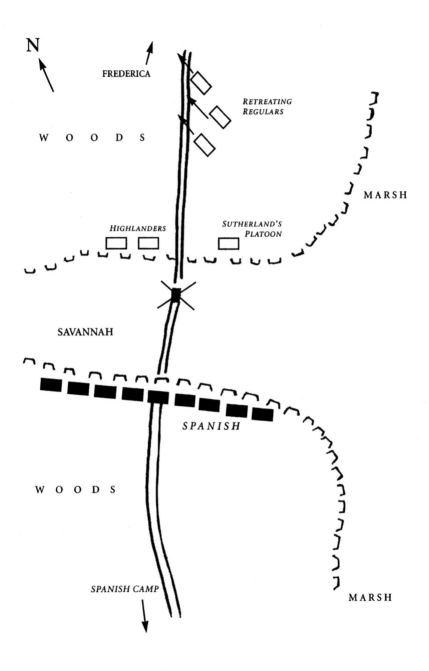

N

FREDERICA

RETREATING
REGULARS

W   O   O   D   S

MARSH

HIGHLANDERS

SUTHERLAND'S
PLATOON

SAVANNAH

SPANISH

W   O   O   D   S

MARSH

SPANISH CAMP

BATTLE OF BLOODY MARSH, PHASE II

THE GRENADIER

In 18th Century armies, one company of each regiment was composed of an elite group of soldiers known as grenadiers. The name stemmed from a bygone day when certain soldiers were selected to throw grenades in combat. Early grenades were fickle things to handle, and the grenade throwers were normally grouped into separate units to keep the other ranks out of harm's way. Since tall, long armed men could hurl grenades a greater distance than could average sized soldiers, grenadiers were chosen for size as well as courage, and the grenadier company literally loomed head and shoulders above the other units. These splendid troops were so impressive that even after technological advances in grenade development had made them obsolete as bomb throwers, grenadiers were retained as an elite segment of each regiment. They were now armed, equipped, and uniformed as standard infantrymen, except for their headgear. To further extend their considerable height, they wore towering hats, a foot or more tall, thereby enhancing the awe and fear experienced by the beholder. Oglethorpe's six-company regiment did not initially contain a grenadier company, but one was added just prior to the Spanish invasion. The two Spanish regiments deployed on St. Simons each contained a grenadier company.

been killed. However, the continuing sound of musket fire contradicted this report, and Oglethorpe managed to turn most of them around to follow him back to the fray. Captain Demere and Ensign Gibbon obeyed his order and helped restore the shattered unit, but a third officer, whose name went unrecorded, disobeyed his commander and continued back to Frederica.[6]

By the time Oglethorpe and the rallied troops reached the site of the engagement, the battle was over. He noted the "great many dead"[7] along the causeway, and he counted among the casualties a Spanish officer who one of the prisoners claimed was Captain Barba, the column commander. In reality it was the dying Ensign Burcardi.

So ended the Battle of Bloody Marsh. Over the following years the size of the forces engaged and the number of Spanish casualties grew with the telling until the marsh turned red with Spanish blood. In reality it was a rather modest affair. Oglethorpe missed it completely, and half his troops turned and ran after the first volley. But Lieutenant Sutherland's display of courage, tenacity, and leadership under fire brighten the annals of British military history, and the battle marked the high water mark of the Spanish challenge to England's American colonies.

❖   ❖   ❖

THE MARSH

CHAPTER IX

AFTERMATH

SOON AFTER HIS arrival on the battlefield of Bloody Marsh, Oglethorpe was joined by the other two line companies of the 42nd Regiment of Foot. He led his reinforced echelons down the military road to a position just short of the Spanish camp where they could intercept any Spanish stragglers who had not yet reached their own lines. Here the British spent the night, for Oglethorpe hoped to disperse the invaders with an early morning surprise attack. At daybreak he sent his Indian allies forward to scout the enemy positions. They returned to report the Spanish troops were well dug in and supported by the guns of warships lying off shore.[1] They estimated the Spanish numbers to be in excess of four thousand. This estimate was high, of course, but it appears to have been accepted by Oglethorpe without question or subsequent modification.

Deeming the odds too great to justify an assault on the Spanish camp, Oglethorpe and his command returned to Frederica for a much-needed rest. He placed the officer who had showed cowardice under arrest pending court martial, and he rewarded those who had exhibited valor. Lieutenant Charles Mackay was named aide-de-camp, and Lieutenant John Sutherland was promoted to major. Later in the day, on that 8th of July, the British cause received another boost with the arrival from Jekyll Island of Horton and his company of grenadiers, together with the better part of two companies of regulars.

During the next three days Oglethorpe continued to strengthen his defenses and refurbish his forces, while Montiano was beset by nagging doubts as his troubles mounted. Events had convinced the Spanish commander that another advance up the military road would be futile, and repeated attempts by his Indian scouts to find an alternate route to Frederica were fruitless. Maintaining an adequate water supply continued to be a problem. Indians ambushed a party of sailors in search of water and killed two of its number, almost within sight of the Spanish camp.[2] Oglethorpe's Indians also made the manning of defensive outposts a dreaded duty. Feuding broke out between the Havana units and soldiers from the St. Augustine garrison, and the horseless dragoons quarreled with the infantry.

Stragglers from the Gully Hole Creek disaster who had fled through the forest continued to arrive exhausted and torn by underbrush. One of the last to stagger in, after spending two nights in the woods, was Captain Hernandez. He became something of a hero when he described how he had been captured but had disarmed and killed two guards with their own weapons in order to escape. English documents reported no such incident.

Montiano knew that a British naval flotilla was at Charleston, and his anxiety over its possible appearance off St. Simons increased with each passing day. Each day also carried him deeper into the hurricane season, and a hurricane was a greater threat to a sea-borne expedition than was an enemy fleet. To make matters worse, his quartermaster informed Montiano that only a dozen or so days of supply were left. Allowing for a six-day return journey, this meant only six days remained for him to defeat the British on St. Simons. Finally, he was ever haunted by Governor de Guemes' instructions to send the Havana garrison home intact and as soon as possible.[3]

On July 9th Montiano called a council of war to discuss the situation and elicit recommendations from his senior subordinates. Stemming from these deliberations was the decision to try and land the army closer to Frederica, thus avoiding the dreaded forests that blanketed the island. A naval reconnaissance force of three warships, under command of Navy Lieutenant Don Adrian Cantein, proceeded up the Frederica River, charged with finding a suitable landing site and sounding the channels to determine if they were deep enough to allow passage of the larger ships.

The waterway left solid ground at Gascoigne Bluff and wound its way through the marsh for some distance, then doubled back to skirt the island for a few hundred yards before swinging back into the marsh. At the far end of this solid ground sat the bastion of Frederica. Cantein determined the waterway was deep enough to accommodate the Spanish fleet, and he found the landing site he sought. Capable of accommodating the whole Spanish army, it was solid open ground that extended right up to the walls of Frederica. But there was a catch. Forces from Frederica would surely oppose any landing there, and the landing would have to be conducted under cannon fire from the fort. In fact, Cantein was unable to approach the solid ground because he came under intense fire from mortar and cannon batteries guarding the approaches to Frederica.[4] Although they were well within range of the guns, none of the Spanish ships were hit. Perhaps the cannons were manned

VOLLEY FIRE

Troops firing their muskets in unison produced a great shock effect, as well as a devastating storm of lead. All armies tried to deliver the first volley in this manner. Subsequent firing could also take this form, normally delivered by platoon formations, but the variances in the time required for different soldiers to reload their weapons in the heat of battle led more often to individual delivery of fire after the initial volley. But that first volley was important, and the timing of it was critical. As opposing forces, arrayed in dressed ranks, came within range of one another, each commander had to perform a continuing time-distance evaluation as he prepared to give the command to fire. The side that delivered the first volley gained an important advantage in that fewer of the enemy remained to shoot back. But once those muskets were discharged, several critical seconds were required to reload, and all during that time the advancing enemy was cutting down the range (and thereby increasing the accuracy) of their first volley. If the separating distance was short enough, a rushing bayonet charge might decide the issue before anyone could reload. Finally there was the psychological effect of standing with an empty musket in the face of a determined enemy assault. At such times a small voice shouted in the soldier's ear, "Never mind reloading! Run!' Only a well-trained man could resist that advice. The wooded terrain of the New World discouraged the delivery of volley fire, but it was the initial British volley that decided the Battle of Bloody Marsh.

by the same gunners who were at Fort Saint Simons when the Spanish fleet ran by it.

The naval reconnaissance force returned to the Spanish camp on the afternoon of July 10th, and on the 11th the Spanish Indian allies resumed the unrewarding search for another land route to Frederica. The following day Oglethorpe was ready to take the offensive. Receiving information about the deplorable state of Spanish moral, he determined the time was ripe for an early morning surprise attack on the Spanish camp.[5] That night he led a force of over four hundred troops to the vicinity of the Spanish outposts. Early the next morning as the soldiers were stealthily moving into assault positions a curious thing occurred. A musket suddenly discharged. It was carried by a Frenchman, presumably one of the sailors Oglethorpe had drafted for service from the merchant ships marooned at Frederica by the Spanish attack. The aroused Spanish soldiers sprang to arms and manned their defenses, and the Frenchman ran for protection to the Spanish lines.[6]

Having lost the element of surprise, Oglethorpe called off the attack, but he conducted a noisy demonstration to jangle Spanish nerves. Oglethorpe knew the Frenchman would provide Montiano with a full report of the English strength, so he sought to discredit the report by convincing the Spanish that the Frenchman was a double agent. To accomplish this, he paid a sum of money to a prisoner to return to the Spanish camp and deliver a message to the Frenchman, correctly anticipating the letter would be intercepted by Spanish authorities, The letter, written in French, appeared to be from a friend who assured the Frenchman that the promised money had been delivered and that it would be doubled if he could lead a Spanish patrol into a trap that had been set for it. The somewhat heavy-handed ruse did not fool the Spanish, but the Frenchman's report confirmed Montiano's worst fears. The informer somewhat over estimated Oglethorpe's available manpower, but he did provide a fairly accurate description of the defensive works guarding Frederica. He also reported Oglethorpe was expecting reinforcements from the north.[7] It was actually more a hope than an expectation, but it coincided with what Montiano believed and dreaded most.

By now the discouraged Montiano was looking for an honorable excuse to terminate the expedition and return home. The excuse came the very next afternoon in the form of five ships which appeared on the horizon.[8] They had been sent by Governor Bull from Charleston to find out what was afoot on St. Simons. Spotting the Spanish flag planted over the island's southern fortifications, they turned and sailed back to Charleston. To Montiano these ships appeared to be the advance echelon of an English fleet bent on trapping the Spanish in St. Simons Sound.

The Spanish completed the destruction of Fort St. Simons and its surrounding defense works, burned the houses in the vicinity, loaded the captured British cannon, and embarked for home. The Havana contingent put out to sea and sailed directly to Cuba. Montiano and the St. Augustine garrison were transferred to Jekyll Island to march down the length of the island, destroying English buildings and supplies as they went. At the southern end they were met by boats which transferred them to Cumberland Island. Here they found the abandoned Fort St. Andrew and a number of horses left behind when its garrison departed. The Spanish destroyed the fort and slaughtered the horses. They then continued on to deal with Fort William on the southern end of the island.

Isolated, outnumbered, and without knowledge of what had transpired on St. Simons, the Fort William garrison might well have assumed the worse and surrendered without offering any resistance. However, an English force in small boats had followed the Spanish, and Oglethorpe was able to get a message to the fort assuring its commander, Lieutenant Alexander Stuart, that help was on the way. Stuart and the garrison put up a spirited defense, and after three hours the Spanish broke off the siege and sailed for home. So ended the Spanish expedition to destroy Georgia and ravish South Carolina.

Oglethorpe barely paused to savor his victory before returning to the task of strengthening his defenses. He was convinced the Spanish would return with a larger force to resume the contest. Although he realized it would take several months to get reinforcements from England, he nevertheless applied for additional forces. He received some well-deserved praise from the mother country, but no troops.

However, Montiano had no plans to resume the contest. He was content to return to St. Augustine and compose his report to the King of Spain. It was a masterpiece. In the report he did not refer directly to his failure to accomplish his mission, but blamed his inability to achieve all he had hoped for on the "Hand of God," which had directed the disruptive storm. He then went on to proclaim the expedition a resounding success by enumerating its accomplishments: the destruction of two forts, the capture of war material, the burning of buildings, the taking of two merchant ships, etc.—all carried out with dispatch and few casualties. Then, with breathtaking audacity, he concluded by suggesting the King generously reward his achievements.

"I expect of the royal magnanimity of your majesty, that it will deign to regard itself well served in the operations under consideration, and that I shall have the satisfaction of receiving honors from Your Majesty, whose Catholic royal person I pray our Lord to preserve as many happy days as Christendom may need.

St. Augustine in Florida, August 3, 1742.
Don Manuel de Montiano"[9]

The King did not shower him with honors, but Montiano retained his position as Governor of Florida.

There would be no follow-up Spanish invasion of Georgia. Spain had had enough of the contest and had resigned itself to accepting the status quo. The St. Marys River was recognized as the southern border of Georgia, as it remains today. However, the War of Austrian Succession, née The War of Jenkin's Ear, dragged on. The following year, 1743, Oglethorpe led another military foray to Florida. It was a small one, compared to his earlier adventure, and it did not accomplish much.

Later that same year Oglethorpe was accused, unjustly, of a number of shortcomings and had to return to England to clear his name and face court martial charges brought by his former executive officer, Lieutenant Colonel Cook. There were a total of nineteen charges, the most serious of which was the accusation that Oglethorpe had required his soldiers to pay for rations which had been issued free.[10] He was cleared of all charges and the disgruntled Cook was dismissed from the service, but Oglethorpe never returned to the colony he had founded and guided through its formative years. He married late in life and lived on to the ripe old age of 89. He died in 1785, having lived long enough to see his colony of Georgia become a state in that pugnacious new entity known as the United States of America.

The War of Austrian Succession finally ended in 1748, and with the return of peace, the threat to Georgia and the Carolinas vanished. No longer needed to guard the frontier, the 42nd Regiment of Foot was disbanded. Some of the veterans returned to England, but a large number of them settled in Georgia on land granted for their services by King George II.[11] Many of the residents of southeast Georgia today can trace their ancestry to these soldiers.

One company of British regulars was retained to man the Frederica fortifications. With the departure of the regiment, the settlement at Frederica withered as many of its citizens drifted away to other locations. A fire destroyed what remained of the town in 1758.[12]

CHAPTER X

MYSTERIES AND HEROES

By comparing the English and Spanish accounts of the 1742 campaign, a logical and complete chronology of events can be drawn, although there remain some unanswered questions, a few unresolved points of debate, and certain contradictions that invite comment. For example, a case can be made that the site of the Battle of Bloody Marsh is other than that indicated by current historical markers. The open savanna lying between the opposing forces has long disappeared, a victim of human development and shifting marshlands. There are other points along the marsh that would also fit the time-distance restrictions of the event, but the site now marked by the National Park Service was chosen only after careful research.

Another point of debate is the actual size of the English fortification on the southern end of St. Simons Island. The Spanish describe the installation as a collection of small fortifications and battery positions, but there exists a plan for a massive fortress larger than the bastion at Frederica. Had such a fortress existed at the time of the Spanish invasion, it is doubtful if it would have been abandoned by the British, and even more doubtful if the Spanish fleet could have sailed past it relatively unscathed. It is unlikely we will ever know for sure, because all traces of the ruins were lost to the sea over the years. We do know that, whatever its size, the fortification was a spectacular failure. Indeed, one of the minor mysteries of the campaign is how the Spanish fleet managed to pass, in single file, down a known channel, in close proximity to British guns, without losing a single ship. The answer is probably a combination of Spanish luck and poor English marksmanship. The shortcomings of English gunners is understandable, however, since a high degree of proficiency in firing 18th Century cannons was only achieved through practice and a significant expenditure of training ammunition. Ammunition was expensive, and Oglethorpe's resources simply would not support much practice.

THE FATE OF THE FLEEING OFFICER

One of the unanswered questions concerning the Battle of Bloody Marsh is what happened to the British officer who not only fled the scene of battle, but disobeyed Oglethorpe's order to turn back and fight. Oglethorpe mentioned the incident in his letter to Newcastle: "I ordered them (the fleeing men) to halt and march back against the Enemy which orders Captain Demere and Ensign Gibbon obeyed but another officer did not but made the best of his way to town..."[1] He did not name the officer, although in the same letter he named and condemned a Lieutenant Tolson for turning back when his boat load of soldiers was pursued by a Spanish warship off Cumberland Island. Certainly desertion in the face of the enemy and disobeying a direct order were more serious offenses. If ever there was a soldier who deserved severe punishment, it was this unnamed officer, yet no record exists of his ever having been tried or punished. His identity and fate remain hidden to this day.

The errant officer may have come from a family so influential that Oglethorpe and the Georgia colony simply could not risk its ill will. Power politics and family influence played large parts in the conduct of British affairs in the 1700's, as they do today, and Oglethorpe was well attuned to them. The officer in question may have been quietly shipped home as everyone celebrated the Spanish defeat and tried hard to forget the embarrassing flight of a company of British Red Coats.

THE LOST CAPTAINS

Apparently captains were held in higher regard in the 18th Century then they are today, because they were listed separately from the lower ranks on casualty lists. The English claimed to have captured one and killed two others, although Spanish records show only one captain captured. One of the captains can be accounted for in the death of Ensign Bucardi immediately following the Battle of Bloody Marsh. Perhaps to cater to what his captors wanted to hear, one of the Spanish soldiers taken prisoner at that battle identified the dying officer as Captain Barba, commander of the Spanish column.

The second Spanish captain pronounced dead by the British was Captain Hernandez, who was with the ill-fated Spanish reconnaissance party defeated at Gully Hole Creek. He was the one who staggered into the Spanish camp with the story that he had killed his two captors. English records make no mention of two dead prisoner guards. A possible explanation is that both the English and Spanish were capable of bending the truth somewhat. The following is offered as a possible scenario to explain the mystery:

TRAINING MANUALS

Troop training consisted primarily of close order drill and by-the-numbers weapon loading exercises. The non-commissioned officers conducted most of the training, but the officers were expected to be present, if for no other reason than to decipher the British training manuals which made their appearance in the 18th Century to promote uniformity of effort. Even back then, military writing was ponderous. Take for example this excerpt from *The New Highland Military Discipline,* published in 1757:

You turn upon your heels as upon springs, all your Right-toes to the Rear, and the Left will be across your own Lines, at the same time you turn the Heels, you turn the Firelock as Lightning along with them, catching it on the Ball and two last fingers of your Right-hand, holding the Cartouch betwixt your finger and thumb; carefully you load with Cartouch as directed. As soon as the Rammers are returned, take fast hold of the Muzzel of your Piece, instead of putting your fingers across the Mouth for fear of Accidents, which very often happens, by a Piece going off; after which you turn on your Heels and the Firelock into the hollow of your Right-side at the same time, you proceed to fire by the Words of Command; in this method of Standing you have no Occasion to kneel down to fire; but if your Commanding Officer chuse it, you may kneel without the least loss of Time, and remember you are to put your Left-foot forward, and not your Right-foot backwards, as usual; for that always discommodes the Rear Ranks, and has always been a Complaint amongst the Men, by keeping them a Muttering one at another, which ought not to be.[ix]

Hernandez was taken prisoner, along with Captain Sanchez, in the initial onrush of rangers, Indians, and Highlanders that overwhelmed the lead elements of the Spanish column. On his way to the rear under guard, Hernandez suddenly broke for the woods and was well on his way before the startled guards could cock their muskets and fire at him. They obviously missed, but they may have thought, or perhaps imagined, they had mortally wounded him. At any rate, neither of them relished the thought of returning empty handed and admitting to Oglethorpe that they had allowed an unarmed prisoner to escape. Instead, they reported their prisoner had been killed in an attempt to escape, reasoning that a lost dead captain was almost as good as a captured live one. The British guards were not the only ones to avoid censure by concocting a tall tale. Having suffered defeat and the loss of his command, Hernandez undoubtedly dreaded the reception he would receive when he reached the Spanish camp. To soften the expected condemnation, he made up the story of disarming and killing his captors with their own weapons. He reasoned that his claim would be unverifiable under the circumstances, and a tale of personal bravado might even turn him into a hero. And so it did. By the time Hernandez reached camp, the Spanish needed a hero to brighten an otherwise gloomy situation. Hernandez fit the bill. Montiano cited the brave captain's audacity in his letter to the King.

THE MYSTERIOUS FRENCHMAN

Of the figures that played key roles during the Spanish campaign on St. Simons, none is more intriguing than the mysterious Frenchman whose musket discharge alerted the Spanish and spoiled the British attack on July 13th. He is mentioned, but not named, in both the English and Spanish accounts. The Spanish described him only as "a deserter," and Oglethorpe's reference told little more: "A French Man who, without my knowledge, was come down amongst the Volunteers, fired his gun and deserted."[2] Where did he come from? Was he really a Spanish spy or merely a clever deserter? Or was he neither? The latter seems most likely. The chances are he was an innocent third-country national who found himself in the wrong place at the wrong time. Consider the following possibility:

The Frenchman was a crewmember of a merchant ship, one of a number of "volunteer" merchant crewmen drafted by Oglethorpe to serve as musketeers. 18th Century ships, even British men-o-war, carried crews that frequently included foreign nationals. As a Frenchman, it is doubtful if he had much affection for the English, but as a common seaman, there was nothing much he could do about being pressed into service. This would account for him being in the forest outside the Spanish camp on that fateful morning.

The discharge of the musket was probably an accident. The musket firing mechanism may have been tripped into the "full-cock"[3] position when the troops deployed through the thick underbrush. Once the piece was fully cocked, dropping it, or even brushing the trigger, could result in a discharge. Accidental or not, that discharge obviously doomed the planned surprise attack and assured a stiff punishment for the one responsible when he got back to Frederica. It probably dawned on the Frenchman that he would be better off among the Spanish than with the English, so he ran for the security of the Spanish camp.

And so it was that an unknown French seaman made a brief appearance on history's stage to earn the wrath of the British and, through an act of carelessness, to spare the lives of countless English and Spanish soldiers. Events proved that the impending attack would have been superfluous to the outcome of the campaign. The Spanish were on the verge of departing anyway, and the attack would only have resulted in a number of unnecessary casualties. Ironically, that poor Frenchman should have been celebrated as a hero by both sides.

THE HERO

Before leaving the subject of heroes, we should pause to consider the accomplishments of the one true hero to emerge from the contest: Lieutenant John Sutherland. One of the most difficult tasks that can be faced by a military leader is to turn back panic-stricken soldiers who are fleeing from the enemy. Once a unit is seized by panic, fear feeds upon itself to hurl soldiers into an unreasoned stampede to the rear. To stem such a flight, a leader must possess an uncommon amount of courage, determination, and strength of character. The heroic performance of Sutherland and two sergeants at the Battle of Bloody Marsh not only restored the left side of the British line, it also salvaged the reputation of the 42nd Regiment of Foot. Oglethorpe recognized the significance of what they had done and rewarded them accordingly. He did not say much about the incident in his letter to Newcastle, mentioning only that upon his arrival on the battlefield of Bloody Marsh, "I found one platoon of the regiment under command of Lieutenant Sutherland...," but he also stated further along in the letter, "I appointed Lieutenant Sutherland Brigade major."[4]

Had there been a leadership trophy presented at the end of hostilities, it most certainly would have gone to John Sutherland.

❖   ❖   ❖

CHAPTER XI

THE MANY FACES OF BLOODY MARSH

PERHAPS THE GREATEST mystery associated with the Spanish invasion is how the Battle of Bloody Marsh became so distorted in later history books. Contemporary reports of the campaign are largely limited to two documents written shortly after the event by the opposing commanders. Oglethorpe's narration is contained in a long letter written to the Duke of Newcastle in which he describes events as seen through British eyes in general and Oglethorpe's eyes in particular. Montiano wrote a similar letter to the Spanish King, appropriately glossing over certain shortcomings. His report is supplemented and reinforced by a day-to-day journal kept by one of his senior staff officers. Montiano's letter closely coincides with this journal, and it is remarkably similar to Oglethorpe's report. There are differences, of course, but most of them occur in the areas of troop strengths and casualties. All soldiers tend to overestimate the size of the enemy and exaggerate the number of casualties the enemy suffers.

Here we note that there was another contemporary description of Bloody Marsh attributed to John Sutherland, one of only two British officers who were present throughout the battle. It was published in the London Gazette in December 1742. Unfortunately it was a third person account which closely followed Oglethorpe's report. It downplayed the panic that seized the English troops, overestimated Spanish casualties, and barely mentioned the Red Coat platoon that stood its ground at the side of the Highlanders.

Reconstructing the military events as they transpired on St. Simons in 1742 was difficult for 19th Century American historians and biographers because of the paucity of English records covering the subject and the absence of English translations of Spanish accounts. Many writers barely touched upon the military aspects of the subject before hurrying on to better-documented areas. Henry Bruce devoted less than a page of his 284 page biography of Oglethorpe to the Battle of Bloody Marsh,[1] and Amos Ashbach

Ettinger used a single paragraph to cover the battle in his book, *James Edward Oglethorpe, Imperial Idealist*.[2] Kenneth Coleman was even more cautious. In his *Colonial Georgia, A History*, he devoted only three short sentences to the event:

> On July 7 Spanish troops marched against Frederica and were driven back by Oglethorpe's men. There were several other attacks and counterattacks. When the day's fighting ended the Spanish were back at their camp at Ft. Saint Simons under the protection of their cannon. (sic) [3]

Other writers were more expansive. A typical expanded narration was provided by William Bacon Stevens in Volume I of his *History of Georgia*.

> (The Spanish) stacked their arms and yielded themselves to repose. Sutherland and Mackay. who from their hiding places had anxiously watched all their movements, now raised the signal of attack —- a Highland cap upon a sword —- and the soldiers poured in on the unsuspecting enemy a well delivered and most deadly fire. Volley succeeded volley, and the sand was strewn with the dead and dying. A few of the Spanish officers attempted, though in vain, to reform their broken ranks; discipline was gone orders were unheeded; safety alone was sought, and when, with a Highland shout of triumph, the platoon burst among them with leveled bayonet and flashing claymore, The panic stricken foe fled in every direction —- some to the marsh, where they were mired and taken —- some along the defile, where they were met by the tomahawk and broadsword —- and some into the thicket, where they became entangled and lost; and a few only escaped to camp. . . .[4]

Caroline Couper Lowell in her *The Golden Isles of Georgia* promoted the lieutenants Mackay and Sutherland to the rank of captain and gave "Captain" Sutherland command of the Red Coat company. She went on to say, "Upon a signal a heavy fire was opened on the Spaniards who were thrown into the utmost confusion. . . many were hunted down by the Indians who, on hearing the firing, had come on a run to be in on the death. The marsh was covered by the dead and dying. . . ."[5]

In summarizing the history of St. Simons Island, R. Edwin Green provided a clue as to how the Battle of Bloody Marsh got its name. "So many

---

ELSEWHERE IN THE WORLD

During the three-year period, 1740 - 1743, while the struggle for Georgia was in progress, elsewhere in the world:

Frederick the Great of Prussia came to the throne, introduced freedom of the press and freedom of worship to Prussia, and fought the First Silecian War against Maria Theresa of Austria; Handel composed "The Messiah;" and in Philadelphia Benjamin Franklin founded "The General Magazine." Voltaire wrote the tragedy "Mohomet;" Boucher painted "The Bath of Diana;' and the Royal Military Academy was established in Woolwich, England. Vitus Bering died of cold and hunger after discovering the straight that bears his name; English cotton factories opened in Birmingham and Northampton; Nathanael Greene, American Revolutionary general, was born; and Anders Celcius, a Swiss astronomer invented the centigrade thermometer.

Two hundred and fifty years had elapsed since Columbus first landed in the New World. Two hundred years later the Japanese attack on Pearl Harbor would launch the United States into World War II.[x]

Spaniards were killed that the marsh was said to have turned red from their blood. About five hundred Spanish soldiers were killed, wounded, or taken prisoner at the Battle of Bloody Marsh. . . ."[6] Bernice McCullar, in her book, *This Is Your Georgia*, as to the naming the battle, quoted two of the participants. "Captain (sic) Mackay had told them (the British troops), 'When I hold up my cap on the end of my gun, that will be the signal for you to attack the Spaniards.' He held up his cap; the English soldiers from Georgia, with their Indian allies, rushed to the attack. They caught the Spanish by surprise, and the ground at the battle site was strewn with the wounded and the dead.

"'What a bloody marsh,' somebody said. The site became known as the 'Bloody Marsh'. . . ."[7]

Children's books also carried expanded versions of the battle, with hundreds of Spanish casualties and a marsh that turned red with their blood. Joyce Blackburn, an author of children's books, painted a particularly stirring picture of the battle for her young readers in her biography of Oglethorpe.

(The Indians) passed from tree to tree moving nearer the edge of the wood. The Highlanders, as much at home in the forest as their "native" friends, crawled silently forward. Unaware and off guard, the Latins laughed and joked, hearing nothing. But one of their horses either heard a sound or glimpsed a sudden shaft of light off the highly polished shield of an approaching Scot. The animal whinnied and reared.... The British, trained in guerrillalike tactics of the Indians, rushed whooping from all directions, firing point blank into the mass of enemy troops. The attack was at such close range the Indians could send their tomahawks straight at faces and necks unprotected by heavy Spanish armor while giant Scots plunged bayonets and dirks into every full belly they could catch....[8]

These fanciful accounts of the battle carry common threads —- the ambush, the Highland cap raised on a sword, the slaughter, etc. —- that suggest they stem from a common source. A review of old publications indicates this was the case. The first published deviation from reports written at the time of the battle was recorded by a Captain Hugh McCall early in the 19th Century. Captain McCall was a Revolutionary War veteran who came to Georgia not long after that war and wrote one of the earliest histories of the region. His descriptions of the battles of Gully Hole Creek and Bloody Marsh were fairly accurate, although he referred to neither of the encounters by the name we call it today. But then he added a third battle to the narrative. He told of the entire Spanish army setting out in a final attack on Frederica. On the way the Spanish troops were ambushed by the British and driven back with great loss of life.[9]

Apparently the source of his information were the old veterans of the battle. Several lived in the area when McCall first came to Georgia, and old veterans can always be counted upon to spice up the narratives of bygone glories. We should also note there was very little in the way of contemporary writing to contradict flights of fantasy on the part of veterans. In those days the vast majority of enlisted soldiers could not write, and nearly all the British officers involved had performed in less than exemplary fashion and had good reason not to leave a record of what happened. The void of written records invited imaginative stories.

We know for sure old veterans were the source of the account published by the Georgia Historical Society in 1840.[10] The piece was written by Thomas Spaulding who had grown up on St. Simons Island and, as a boy, had roamed the sites of the island battles and listened to the stories of the veterans, who must have been quite elderly at the time. Spaulding wrote of advancing Spanish troops stopping to cook a meal and being quietly surrounded by the British. In this account, an alert Spanish horse was the first to spot the ambush and whinny an alarm. But the warning came too late. A Highland cap was raised on a bayonet as a signal to open fire, and devastating salvos turned the savanna into a scene of carnage.

Spaulding freely admitted his description of the Battle of Bloody Marsh was based on stories told by old veterans, but he proffered the story as fact. Then, perhaps to rationalize its divergence from Oglethorpe's account, he suggested the recollections, stretching back many years, of those who had been at the scene were somehow more to be trusted than records written immediately after the battle. He wrote:

> In details that have been given of that day,
> written probably in a hurry, and certainly not
> by one himself engaged in that action, there is
> some confusion of position, and some mingling
> of events, which can only be understood by one
> familiar in his childhood with the scene, and
> who has traveled it over often with more than
> one who was himself an actor in the conflict.[11]

It was Spaulding's account of the battle that provided the major source of information for later historians and biographers who have given us the romantic versions of the Battle of Bloody Marsh. But perhaps these writers should be forgiven. After all, Spaulding was a respected historian, and if writers are given a choice of providing a dull official account of a battle or one with a little more color and action, they will almost always choose the latter.

❖   ❖   ❖

"We are resolved not to suffer defeat . . . "
                                              James Oglethorpe

"I expect of the royal magnanimity of your majesty, that it will deign to regard itself well served . . . "
                                              Don Manuel de Montiano

CHAPTER XII

THE LEADERS

Evaluation of military commanders from the comfortable perch of hindsight has long been a favorite pastime for students of military history. As we indulge in this pastime, there is always the temptation to judge the losing general as inferior and condemn him for his mistakes, while lavishing praise on the winner, who by virtue of his victory is deemed the better of the two. This is not always accurate, however. Montiano and Oglethorpe were fairly evenly matched in overall ability. The former was probably not as incompetent as he is often depicted, and the latter not quite as competent.

MONTIANO

Don Manuel de Montiano was a professional soldier who exhibited energy and ability in preparing for the war with England. A realist and a conservative, he wisely drew his outnumbered troops into the Castillo de San Marcos when Oglethorpe invaded Florida, and he resisted all attempts to lure him out to fight in the open. Yet when the opportunity arose, he was ready to gamble on a bold move to destroy the British force at Fort Mosa. He displayed the same calculated audacity when he ran the gauntlet of English guns to obtain a suitable landing spot in the campaign of 1742. Prior to that time, he had also proven to be a lucky general. Critical reinforcements reached him just before the British arrived to lay siege to St. Augustine in 1740; vital supplies slipped through the British blockade just as his last stores of food were being consumed; and two years later he sailed past the guns of Fort St. Simons without losing a single ship. Then his luck ran out.

Montiano has been faulted for not being more aggressive and enterprising in his attempt to reach the fortifications of Frederica, but there was not much more he could do. A pair of bloody setbacks the day after landing proved the folly of attempting to force a passage through the tangled forests covering St. Simons Island. Marshes and well-placed batteries discouraged an amphibious approach. Actually there were few options open to him. A bolder general might have rallied his forces for a daring thrust up the Inland Waterway to effect a night landing near the walls of Frederica, and it might have worked. Oglethorpe would probably have tried it. However it would have resulted in many casualties, and the odds against it succeeding were formidable.

From the very beginning time ran against Montiano. The threat of British naval interference increased with each passing day, supplies ran low, morale deteriorated, and the chances of a hurricane mounted as the season progressed. Taking full council of his growing fears, Montiano was quite ready to break off the campaign when the ships from Charleston appeared on the horizon. By then there was little else left for him to do.

OGLETHORPE

Although Oglethorpe had never led troops in battle, he had served with the Austrian army in the Turkish campaign and was the logical choice to lead the British forces during the war with Spain. His military performance during that period has largely been overshadowed and eclipsed by his achievements as a colonial administrator. As a field commander he had his faults. The South Carolina investigation into the failure of the Florida expedition unequivocally laid the blame for the fiasco on Oglethorpe,[1] but the charge was not entirely fair. Many others, particularly the British naval commander, should have shared the blame. Nevertheless, much of the criticism leveled by the South Carolinians was accurate.

It was true that Oglethorpe seldom listened to advice from his subordinate commanders, and it was also true that he had a bad habit of forming task forces by throwing together pieces of several different units with scant regard for unit integrity or chain of command. The unit that met its fate at Fort Mosa was a case in point. It was a collection of troops from four different outfits, commanded by two squabbling leaders, and it carried the seeds of its own destruction from the day it was formed.

It was true that the energetic, and often impatient Oglethorpe had trouble delegating authority. It was said he felt he had to do everything himself, to the point of sometimes doing jobs that were properly in the domain of sergeants.[2] This particular shortcoming was evident just prior to the Battle of Bloody Marsh. After deploying his forces, he decided to return to Frederica himself to get reinforcements, rather than sending a deputy, thereby completely missing the battle and, by his absence, contributing to the panic suffered by his soldiers.

At one time or another, Oglethorpe the soldier was also accused of poor judgment, insensitivity, rashness, and vacillation, but there was one thing upon which both his detractors and admirers agreed: he was personally very brave, a courageous commander who led by example. He was the first one to burst into the woods when the Highlanders, rangers, and Indians struck the Spanish column at Gully Hole Creek, and there is little doubt that his example of courage contributed greatly to the British victory.

In the long run, the gods of war do favor the bold over the cautious, the fighter over the calculator; and as the Spanish invasion of St. Simons Island wore on, they sided with Oglethorpe. Yet in the final analysis, it was not leaders or soldiers or guns or battlements that saved Frederica. It was the dense Georgia forest. Filled with interlaced entanglements of vines, thickets, and underbrush, that forest, in all probability, daunted the Spanish as much as did the English defenders. While Montiano was ready to explore the feasibility of landing his forces closer to Frederica, he never risked another advance through the woods after that first attempt.

THE FORT TODAY

A MODERN DAY VISIT

GOLF COURSES, SHOPS, and housing areas have replaced much of the forest that once blanketed St. Simons Island. Where the Spanish fleet fought its way past the guns of Fort St. Simons, giant freighters carrying cargo from around the world now pass from the ocean to the port of Brunswick. Much has changed over the years, but much has remained the same. Brooding live oak trees still watch over the passage of time, and the vast marshes of Glynn separating the island from the mainland have changed not at all.

FORT KING GEORGE

A good place to start our visit to those bygone days is the town of Darien and old Fort King George at the mouth of the Altamaha River. Darien is located 16 miles north of Brunswick on Route 17. A granite marker at the side of the road notes its heritage and honors the Scots who established the town in 1736. Fort King George, which predated the founding by 15 years, is located a mile to the east of the town. A sign points the way.

The fort's original blockhouse succumbed to the elements many years ago, but an authentic replica has been constructed using old records and diagrams. Surrounded by earthen parapets, the restored structure stands overlooking the river at the location of the original fort. The fickle Altamaha River has shifted its main channel further south, but it still sends part of its waters past the site of the stronghold, and on the banks of the river old cemetery stones mark the graves of many of those who died so futilely while manning the fort. Visitors are invited to explore the grounds and examine the blockhouse. Beyond the marsh, five miles or so to the southeast, a line of trees marks the northern reaches of St. Simons Island. Georgia State Park Rangers are on hand to assist visitors and offer information. A small museum in the visitors' center displays relics found in the area and traces the history of Darien.

SAINT SIMONS

Saint Simons Island is only a few water miles from Darien, but to reach it by automobile, we must travel south along Route 17 for about 16 miles to the E. J. Torras Causeway leading to the island. The four mile causeway crosses five bridges as it traverses the Marshes of Glynn, and two of these bridges are high arching structures that provide excellent views of the vast marshes that stretch the length of the Georgia coast and beyond. The roadway reaches the island at Gascoigne Bluff where the Spanish army landed in 1742. Pleasure yachts now stand where Spanish warships once lay at anchor.

We bear right as we reach the island and travel along Kings Way through a tunnel of live oaks for a bit over two miles to the Village of St. Simons. A traffic light at Mallory Street marks the end of Kings Way and the beginning of Ocean Boulevard. Taking a right at the light, we drive down Mallory through the village to park our car by the pier at the end of the street. To the east is Neptune Park, with its towering trees and inviting benches, and on the far side stands the lighthouse where Fort St. Simons once guarded the entrance from the sea. Jekyll Island appears about a mile away to the south.

Standing on the point of land beside the lighthouse, we have a view similar to that of the British gunners on that distant day when they confronted the invading Spanish fleet. And we can trace the passage of that fleet, because the channel of 1742 is much the same as the modern channel, now marked by a line of buoys stretching to the sea. Note the way the channel swings inward toward St. Simons to skirt the shoreline where we are standing.

While at the lighthouse, it is worth our while to walk up the 129 steps coiling along its inner wall to the walkway just below its beacon. The lighthouse is entered through the lighthouse keeper's house, now a museum operated by the Coastal Georgia Historical Society. The view from the top is magnificent, well worth the small entry fee and the 129-step climb.

FREDERICA

To reach the fortified town of Frederica, we follow Ocean View. That is the street running eastward from the center of the village that passes the lighthouse a block to the north. Just beyond the lighthouse, it makes a turn to the left, crosses Ocean Boulevard, and becomes Demere Road. (St. Simon's streets have a bad habit of changing names for no particular reason.) Demere Road, named for the company commander of the Red Coat company at Bloody Marsh, runs northward along the trace of the old Military Road. On this stretch of the street we are retracing the route of the ill-fated Spanish patrols and following the footsteps of the two companies of Spanish grenadiers.

After traveling northward for about a mile and a half, Demere Road gradually bends to the left, passes the site of Bloody Marsh (to which we will return), and heads west. At the next light we turn right onto Frederica Road and follow it up the spine of the island. At a cemetery it bears sharply to the left, crosses a marshy area, and passes historic Christ Church. Just beyond the church is the entrance to Frederica on our left.

The site of Frederica is a Federal Monument operated by the National Park Service. At the visitors' center we can browse through a bookshop run by the Frederica Association, work our way through a small museum, and view a short film before visiting the town of Frederica. Park Rangers are on duty to greet visitors and answer questions,

From the visitors' center we enter the town at the east gate, which is now merely a gap in the long mounds of earth stretching around the town site to the waterway at its western end. These mounds are all that is left of the massive walls that once enclosed the town. Traces of the outer ditch, or moat, can still be seen, dry now except after a heavy rain.

Not much of the fortified town of Frederica remains standing. A portion of the troop barracks lies along the northern reaches of the community, and a fragment of the inner bastion still stands guard on the banks of the inland waterway. The rest of the town long ago succumbed to the elements. However, the English left excellent records that have allowed archeologists to unearth several foundations of the earlier homes. Glassed cases at many of the sites display artifacts found in the area. Information displays provide sketches of the installations and tell of the people who lived there. As we walk down Broad Street, we go by the homes of interpreter Mary Musgrove, ship pilot John Humble, shoemaker John LeValley, and a host of others. Crossing Barracks Street, we pass the residence of entrepreneur John Calwell and see where the Davisons shared a duplex with regimental surgeon Hawkins and his shrewish wife.

At the river's edge we come to the remains of the inner bastion. The raised earthen mounds were once broad ramparts mounting batteries of twelve and eighteen pounder cannon. Parts of the battlements have been lost to erosion, but enough remains to illustrate the dominant presence this fortification once exerted over the adjacent waterway. The 18th Century British flag still flies from the flagpole, and three cannon from that period point southward across the marsh to where Lieutenant Cantien approached on his reconnaissance to find a suitable landing place for the Spanish army. The distant wood line on the left bank of the river marks the high ground he sought, but was unable to reach. Two of the cannons on display are from distant shores, but the center one, a twelve pounder, was probably part of the fortress armament. It was recovered from the river a few yards from where it now stands.

Isolated from the hubbub of the busy island, Frederica National Monument offers a serene setting where the historian and casual visitor alike can wander among towering live oaks and walk with the ghosts of the past.

THE BATTLEFIELDS

The Battlefield of Gully Hole Creek is located about half a mile east of Frederica. As we drive back the way we came, we cross a small bridge spanning Gully Hole Creek, just beyond Christ Church. A few yards to our left (north) is the point where the military road crossed the creek, and just to the right (east) of that point is where the battle took place. A historical marker stands beside the road. A school ground now occupies part of the battle site. The tangled mass of trees, vines and undergrowth covering the path of the stream provides an idea of what the place looked like in 1742 and helps us reconstruct an image of the desperate hand-to-hand struggle that occurred there.

We continue back along Frederica Road, turn left on Demere Road, and return to the site of the Battle of Bloody Marsh. The entrance appears on our left, and there is a small parking area just inside the woods. The site is marked by an information plaque placed by the National Park Service and a stone monument erected by the Society of Colonial Dames and the Georgia Society of Colonial Wars.

The open savanna across which the Spanish grenadiers marched to their destruction has long ago vanished, but the towering trees, draped in somber strands of Spanish moss, provide a setting similar to that occupied by the British soldiers as they awaited the arrival of the Spanish army. If we look closely out across the marsh, we may catch a glimpse of a ghostly column of grenadiers making its way toward where we stand. And if we happen to be in the vicinity on the night of July 7th, perhaps we will hear the drone of distant pipes. It is said that on every field of strife where Highland soldiers fought with great distinction, a ghostly piper appears at midnight on the anniversary of the battle to pipe a salute to his gallant countrymen. If the legend is true, then he surely must pay an annual visit to Bloody Marsh.

❖   ❖   ❖

ENDNOTES FOR TEXT

CHAPTER I

1. Marquess de Casinas, "1742 Journal of the Spanish Expedition Against Georgia Kept by the Marquess of Casinas" *Collections, Georgia Historical Society., Volume VII, part III* (Savannah: The Georgia Historical Society, 1913), p. 67.
2. One ship ran aground and came under intense British cannon fire that killed one man and wounded three others. The ship was later re-floated by the rising tide. Ibid., p.69.

CHAPTER II

1. William Bacon Stevens, *A History of Georgia, Vol. I* (Sanannah: The Beehive Press, 1972), pp. 38–40.
2. R. Edwin Green, *St. Simons Island: A Summary of Its History* (Rome, NY: Arner Publications, 1982), p. 15.
3. Pirates captured and sacked St. Augustine in 1688, thus spurring the construction of the Castillo de San Marcos. *Castillo de San Marcos, Handbook 149* (Washington: National Park Service, n.d.), pp. 5–6.
4. *Castillo,* p. 37
5. Robert Rosen, *A Short History of Charleston, 2nd ed.* (Charleston: The Peninsula Press, 1992), p.17.
6. Buddy Sullivan, *Early Days on the Georgia Tidewater* (Darien, GA: McIntosh County Board of Commissioners, 1990), p. 11.
7. Larry E,. Ivers, *British Drums on the Southern Frontier* (Chapel Hill, NC: The University of North Carolina Press, 1974), pp. 7—8.
8. Stevens, p. 288.

CHAPTER III

1. Francis Moore, *A Voyage to Georgia* (London: n.p., 1744; reprint ed. St. Simons Island: The Fort Frederica Association, 1992), p. 20.
2. Sullivan, p. 17.
3. Amos Aschbach Ettinger, *James Edward Oglethorpe* (Oxford: The Clarington Press, 1936), p. 127. Much of the credit for the excellent relations Oglethorpe forged with the Indians is due his adviser and interpreter, Mary Musgrove. Mary's mother was a Creek Indian, her father a Scot trader. Ibid., p. 134.
4. Until the reign of King George II, British regiments were designated only by the names of their regimental commanders. Colonel J. R. Harper, Forward to *The New Highland Military Discipline of 1757* by George Grant (London: 1757; Alexandria Bay, N.Y.: Museum Restoration Service, 1988), p. 6.

CHAPTER IV

1. Herbert Eugene Bolton and Thomas Maitland Marshall, *1492—1783: The Colonization of North America* (New York: Macmillan Company, 1920; reprint ed. New York: Hafner Publishing Company, 1971), p. 326.
2. Ivers, pp. 103—104.
3. Ibid., p. 127.
4. The coquina, a shell stone native to Florida, was used in the construction of the Castillo de San Marcos. It tended to absorb cannon shot rather than shatter. Michael Gannon, *Florida: A Short History* (Gainesville. FL: University Press of Florida, 1993), p. 15.
5. This Spanish outpost fort is spelled differently in various publications. Here we use the spelling found in early English accounts.
6. According to the practice of the day, those holding royal commissions could command colonial troops, but colonial officers could not command His Majesty's soldiers. Ivers, p. 114.
7. Ibid., p. 123.
8. Ibid., p. 131.

CHAPTER V

1. Aileen Moore Topping, Introduction to reprint of *An Impartial Account of the Late Expedition Against St. Augustine Under General Oglethorpe* (London: Printed for J. Huggonson, in Sword-and-Buckler-Court, over-against the Crown-Tavern on Ludgate-Hill, 1742; Gainesville, FL: University Press of Florida, 1978). pp. xxiii –xxv.
2. Ivers, p. 139.
3. Ibid., pp. 137 & 141.
4. Don Juan Francisco de Guemes y Horcastas, "Letter to Governor Montiano, 14 May, 1742," *Collections, Georgia Historical Society, Vol, VII, part III* (Savannah: The Georgia Historical Society, 1913). P. 28.
5. Ibid.
6. Trevor R. Reese, *Colonial Georgia: A Study in British Imperial Policy in the Eighteenth Century* (Athens, GA: University of Georgia Press, 1963), p. 83.
7. The quotation is found on a stone monument placed at the site of the Battle of Bloody Marsh by the Georgia Society of the Colonial Dames of America and the Georgia Society of Colonial Wars.
8. Ivers, p. 136.
9. Casinas, pp. 67–68.

CHAPTER VI

1. Casinas, pp. 67–69.
2. Essential to the firing of early cannons was a small hole drilled from the top rear of the barrel to the chamber below. A chain of black powder carried the igniting flame down the hole to ignite the powder charge. A cannon could be rendered inoperable by driving a nail, or spike, into this hole, thereby sealing it closed. The process was known as "spiking."
3. Casinas, p. 78.
4. Ibid., p.73.

CHAPTER VII

1. Don Manual de Montiano, "Letter to the King of Spain, dated August 3, 1742," *Collection, Georgia Historical Society, Vol. VII, Part III* (Savannah: The Georgia Historical Society, 1913), p. 91.
2. John Sutherland, "The Battle of Bloody Marsh," *London Gazette*, December 25, 1742.
3. Montiano, p. 91.
4. Ivers, p. 165.

CHAPTER VIII

1. James E. Oglethorpe, "Letter to the Duke of Newcastle describing the Spanish Invasion of Georgia dated July 30, 1742," *Collections of the Georgia Historical Society, Vol. III* (Savannah: The Georgia Historical Society, 1913), p. 136.
2. There is a discrepancy in Spanish reports as to the number of grenadier companies under Barba's command. Casinas reported two companies (Casinas, p.73), but in his report to the King, Montiano claimed he sent three companies of grenadiers to aid the survivors of the morning disaster. (Montiano, p. 91.). The number was probably two, one from each of the two Spanish infantry regiments.
3. Casinas, p. 73.
4. Oglethorpe glossed over the event in his letter to Newcastle describing the action: "Some platoons of ours in the heat of the fight, the air being darkened by smoke and a shower of rain falling, retired in disorder." (Oglethorpe, p. 73.)
5. Casualty figures are Spanish. (Casinas, p. 73.) Contemporary English records did not provide specific numbers of estimated Spanish casualties, a neglect that contributed to some unbridled speculation on the part of future writers.
6. Oglethorpe, p. 136.
7. Ibid.

CHAPTER IX

1. Oglethorpe, p. 136.
2. Casinas, p. 74.
3. Montiano, p. 92.
4. Four mortar rounds and 18 cannon balls were fired at the Spanish ships. (Casinas, p.77.)
5. The basis for Oglethorpe's decision was an unnamed intelligence source in the Spanish camp that reported Spanish morale being very low and that Montiano had lost over 200 men killed. (Oglethorpe, p. 137.)
6. Ibid., pp. 137—138.
7. Montiano, p. 94.
8. Ibid.
9. Ibid., p. 96.
10. Ivers, p. 183
11. Webb Garrison, *Oglethorpe's Folly: The Birth of Georgia* (Lakemont, GA: Copple House Books, 1982), pp. 186—187.
12. Trevor R. Reese, *Frederica: Colonial Fort and Town* (St. Simons Island, GA: Fort Frederica Association, 1969), p. 78.

CHAPTER X

1. Oglethorpe, p. 136.
2. Ibid., pp. 137–138.
3. Loaded muskets were normally carried with the cocking lever drawn back to the half-cock position, which prevented the trigger from being tripped accidentally. When the lever was rotated to the full-cock position, the safety was released, and pressure on the trigger fired the piece.
4. Oglethorpe, pp. 136–137.

CHAPTER XI

1. Henery Bruce, *The Life of Oglethorpe* (New York: Dodd, Mead, and Company, 1890), p. 218.
2. Ettinger, p. 244.
3. Kenneth Coleman, *Colonial Georgia, A History* (New York: Charles Scribner's Sons, 1976) p. 70.
4. Stevens, p pp. 188–189.
5. Caroline Couper Lowell, *The Golden Isles of Georgia* (Atlanta: Cherokee Publishing Company, 1970), p. 49.
6. Green, p 27.
7. Bernice McCullar, *Thie Is Your Georgia* (Mongomery, AL: Viewpoint Publications, Inc., 1972), p. 155.
8. Joyce Blackburn, *James Edward Oglethorpe* (Marietta, GA: R. Bemis Publishing, Ltd., 1994), pp. 140–141.
9. Captain Hugh McCall, *The History of Georgia* (Savannah, n.p., 1811; Atlanta: Cherokee Publishing Company, 1969), p. 129.
10. Thomas Spaulding , "Sketch of the Life of General James Oglethorpe," *Collections of the Georgia Historical Society, Vol. I* (Savannah: The Georgia Historical Society, 1840), pp. 275–280.
11. Ibid., p. 280.

CHAPTER XII

1 An Impartial Account of the Late Expedition Against St. Augustine Under General Oglethorpe (London: Printed for J. Higgonson, in Sword-and-Buckler-Court, over against the Crown-Tavern on Ludgate-Hill, 1742; Gainesville, FL: University Press of Florida, 1978).
2. Ivers, p.136.

ENDNOTES FOR INSERTS

.i Larry E. Ivers, *British Drums on the Southern Frontier* (Chapel Hill, NC: The University of North Carolina Press, 1970), p. 207.

ii Cecil C. P. Lawson, *A History of the Uniforms of the British Army* (London: Norman M Military Publications, Ltd., 1941), p. 93.

iii Major George Hanger, quoted by Anthony D. Darling, *Red Coats and Brown Bess* (Ottawa: Museum Restoration Service, 1970), p. 11.

iv Cannons first came into general use in Europe during the Hundred Years War (1339–1453). Albert Manucy, Artillery Through The Ages (Washington: National Park Service, 1949), p. 3.

v Several companies of American rangers, grouped into a battalion known as Rogers' Rangers, were prominent during the French and Indian War. A daring raid into Quebec against the St. Francis Indians earned these rangers the admiration of even the British regulars. Howard H. Peckham, *The Colonial Wars: 1689 - 1762* (Chicago: The University of Chicago Press, 1974), pp. 160 & 194.

vi Excellent displays of Spanish army uniforms of this period can be seen at the Museo Erjercito (Spanish Army Museum) located two blocks from the Prado in Madrid.

vii All this was changed at the end of the 18th Century when revolutionary France introduced massed armies of citizen soldiers to the battlefields of Europe. Anatol Rapoport, *Editor's Introduction to On War,* by Carl Von Clausewitz (London: Routledge & Kenan Paul, Ltd., 1908; Penquin Books, 1968) p. 20.

viii The Royal Military Academy at Woolwich was opened in 1741. Bernard Grun *The Timetables of History: A Horizontal Linkage of People and Events,* 2nd ed. (New York: Simons and Schuster, 1982), p. 341.

ix Historical Arms Series Number 10: the New Highland Military Discipline of 1757, by George Grant (Alexandria Bay, NY: Museum Restoration Service, 1988), p. 16.

x The Spanish flag flew over Florida for more than 250 years. The American flag will not surpass that record until the mid 21st Century.

BIBLIOGRAPHY

PRIMARY SOURCES

Arrendondo, Antonio de. "Journal of the Spanish Campaign," Collections, Georgia Historical Society, Vol. Part III. Savannah: The Georgia Historical Society, 1913.

Casinas, Marquess de. "Journal of 1742," Collections, Georgia Historical Society, Vol. VII, Part III. Savannah: The Georgia Historical Society, 1913.

Gumese, Don Juan Francisco de. "Letter to Governor Montiano, May 14, 1742," Collections, Georgia Historical Society, Vol. VII, Part III. Savannah: The Georgia Historical Society, 1913.

Montiano, Manual de. "Letter to the King of Spain, August 3, 1742," Collections, The Georgia Historical Society, Vol. VII, Part III. Savannah: The Georgia Historical Society, 1913.

Oglethorope, James E. "Letter to the Duke of Newcastle, July 30, 1742," Collections, The Georgia Historical Society, Vol. VII, Part III. Savannah: The Georgia Historical Society, 1873.

Sutherland, John. "The Battle of Bloody Marsh," as told to a reporter. The *London Gazette*, December 25, 1742.

OTHER SOURCES

Blackburn, Joyce. *James Edward Oglethorpe*. Marietta, GA: R. Bemis Publishing, Ltd.,1994.

Bolton, Herbert Eugene and Marshall, Thomas Maitland. 1492–1738; *The Colonization of North America*. New York: Macmillan Company, 1920; reprint ed. New York: Hafner Publishing Company, 1971.

Bruce, Henry. *The Life of Oglethorpe*. New York: Dodd, Mead and Company, 1890.

Coleman, Kenneth, ed. *A History of Georgia*. Athens, GA: University of Georgia Press, 1977.

Coleman, Kenneth. *Colonial Georgia, A History*. New York: Charles Schribner's Sons.1976.

Darling, Anthony D. *Red Coats and Brown Bess.* Ottawa: Museum Restoration Service, 1970.

Ettinger, Amos Ashbach. *James Edward Oglethorpe, Imperial Idealist.* Hamdon, CN: Archon Books, 1968.

———. *Frederica: Colonial Fort and Town.* St. Simons Island, GA: Fort Frederica Association, 1969.

Gannon, Michael. *Florida: A Short History.* Gainesville, FL: University Press of Florida, 1993.

Garrison, Webb. *Oglethorpe's Folly: The Birth of Georgia* Lakemont, GA: Copple House Books, 1982.

Grant, George. *The New Highland Military Discipline of 1757.* London 1757; Alexandria Bay, NY: Museum Restoration Service, 1988.

Green, R, Edwin. *St. Simons Island: A Summary of Its History.* Rome, NY: Arner Publications, 1992.

Grun, Bernard. *The Timetables of History: A Horizontal Linkage of People and Events,* 2nd ed. New York: Simons and Schuster, 1982.

Harper, J. R., Colonel. Forward to *The New Highland Military Discipline of 1757* by George Grant. London: 1757; Alexandria Bay, NY: Museum Restoration Service, 1988.

Ivers, Larry E. *British Drums on the Southern Frontier.* Chapel Hill, NC: University of North Carolina Press, 1974. NOTE: This is an excellent work, comprehensive and well written.

Johnson, James M. *Militiamen, Rangers and Red Coats, The Military in Georgia, 1754–1776.* Macon, GA: Mercer University Press, 1992.

Jones, Charles C., Jr. *The Dead Towns of Georgia.* Savannah: Morning News Steam Printing House, 1878.

———. *The History of Georgia, Vol. 1.* Cambridge MA: The Riverside Press, 1883

Keegan, John. *A History of Warfare.* New York: Alfred A, Knopf, Inc., 1993.

Lawson, Cecil C. B. *A History of the Uniforms of the British Army.* London: Norman Military Publications, Ltd., 1941.

Lowell, Caroline Couper. *The Golden Isles of Georgia.* Atlanta: Cherokee Publishing Company, 1970.

McCall, Captaon Hugh. *The History of Georgia.* Savannah: n.p., 1811; reprint ed. Atlanta: Cherokee Publishing Company, 1969.

McCullar. *This Is Your Georgia.* Montgomery, AL: Viewpoint Publications, Inc., 1972.

Munucy, Albert. *Artillery Through the Ages.* Washington: National Park Service, 1949.

Moore, Francis. *A Voyage to Georgia*. London: 1744; reprint ed. St Simons Island, GA: Fort Frederica Association, 1992.

Patterson, Howard Leslie. *Arms and Armor in Colonial Georgia, 1526–1783*. Harrisonburg, PA: Stackpole Company, 1956.

Pekham, Howard H. *The Colonial Wars, 1689–1762*. Chicago: The University of Chicago Press, 1964.

Rapoport, Anatol. *Editor's Introduction to On War*. by Carl VonClausewitz. London: Rutledge and Kenan Paul, Ltd., 1908; Penquin Books, 1968.

Reese, Trevor. Colonial Georgia: *A Study in British Imperial Policy in the Eighteenth Century*. Athens, GA: University of Georgia Press. 1963.

Rosen, Robert. *A Short Story of Charleston*. Charleston, SC: Peninsula Press, 1992.

Spaulding, Phinizy and Jackson, Harvey H., ed. *Oglethorpe in Perspective: Georgia's Founder After Two Hundred Years*. Tuscaloosa, AL: University of Alabama Press, 1989.

Spaulding, Thomas. "Sketch of the Life of James Oglethorpe," Collections of the Georgia Historical Society, Vol. I. Savannah: The Georgia Historical Society, 1840.

Stevens, William Bacon. *History of Georgia*. Savannah: Beehive Press, 1972.

Sullivan, Buddy. *Early Days on the Georgia Tidewater*. Darien, GA: McIntosh County Board of Commissioners, 1990.

PAMPHLETS

"Castillo de San Marcos." The Natiional Park Service, U. S. Department of the Interior.

"Fort Frederica." The National Park Service, U. S. Department of the Interior.

"Fort Frederica, A Brief History." The National Park Service, U. S. Department of the Interior.

"The History of Fort King George." Georgia Department of Natural Resouces.

MUSEUM DISPLAY

Museo Ejercito (Spanish Army Museum). Madrid, Spain.

INDEX

About The Author

Jud Conner is a retired Army colonel who commanded every echelon from platoon to brigade during his thirty year military career. He is a graduate of West Point and the National War College, and he holds master's degrees from the University of Florida (Journalism) and The George Washington University (International Affairs). He is the author of four other books: *Vermont from A to Z, Meeting the Press, Alligators Don't Eat Yankees,* and *Southern Yankees and the One-Eyed Alligator.*

He and his wife, Kit, have a home on St. Simons Island.

Buddy Sullivan is the author of numerous studies of the history of Southeast Georgia, among them *Early Days on the Georgia Tidewater*

Animals That Live in the Ocean

Sea Horses

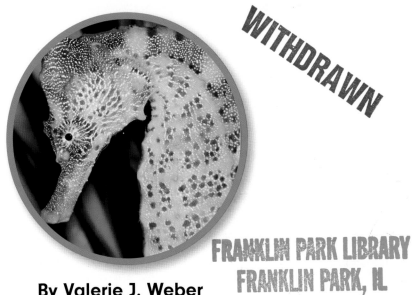

By Valerie J. Weber

Reading Consultant: Susan Nations, M.Ed.,
author/literacy coach/consultant in literacy development

WEEKLY READER®
PUBLISHING

Please visit our web site at www.garethstevens.com.
For a free catalog describing our list of high-quality books,
call 1-800-542-2595 (USA) or 1-800-387-3178 (Canada).
Our fax: 1-877-542-2596

Library of Congress Cataloging-in-Publication Data

Weber, Valerie.
      Sea Horses / by Valerie J. Weber.
          p. cm. — (Animals that live in the ocean)
      Includes bibliographical references and index.
      ISBN-10: 0-8368-9243-7   ISBN-13: 978-0-8368-9243-7 (lib. bdg.)
      ISBN-10: 0-8368-9342-5   ISBN-13: 978-0-8368-9342-7 (softcover)
       1. Sea horses—Juvenile literature. I. Title.
    QL638.S9W43   2009
    597'.6798—dc22   2008013506

This edition first published in 2009 by
Weekly Reader® Books
An Imprint of Gareth Stevens Publishing
1 Reader's Digest Road
Pleasantville, NY 10570-7000 USA

Copyright © 2009 by Gareth Stevens, Inc.

Senior Managing Editor: Lisa M. Herrington
Senior Editor: Barbara Bakowski
Creative Director: Lisa Donovan
Designer: Alexandria Davis
Cover Designer: Amelia Favazza, *Studio Montage*
Photo Researcher: Diane Laska-Swanke

Photo Credits: Cover, pp. 1, 7, 9, 11, 13, 15, 17, 19, 21 © SeaPics.com;
p. 5 © Kristian Sekulic/Shutterstock

Printed in the United States of America

1 2 3 4 5 6 7 8 9 10 09 08

Table of Contents

Boldface words appear in the glossary.

A Puzzling Animal

What has a head like a horse and a tail like a snake? A fish called a sea horse! Sea horses swim in warm oceans around the world.

head

tail

5

A sea horse can be from a half inch to 1 foot long. It has a tiny **crown** on its head. Each sea horse's crown is different.

crown

Bony plates protect the sea horse's body. A thin layer of skin covers the bony plates. The plates look like rings around the animal's body.

plates

Sea horses' **fins** flutter like tiny fans. Sea horses look as if they are flying through the water! They swim slowly, however. A sea horse would take five minutes to swim across a bathtub.

fin

Time for Dinner

A sea horse can wrap its tail around a piece of sea grass. There, the sea horse waits for its food to float past.